SONG OF KATERI:

Princess of the Eucharist

11-05

By Marlene McCauley

*Best Wishes from
the Author
Marlene McCauley*

Grace House Publishing
6237 N. 15th St.
Phoenix, Arizona 85014

Song of Kateri
Princess of the Eucharist

Library of Congress Catalog Number 2005925212
ISBN: 0-9633633-2-8
Library of Congress Copyright Dept.
"Beatification of Kateri Tekakwitha"
Marlene McCauley TX 367-108

Skip Peshak...Computer
Blue River Graphics
Jeani 'Walks-the-Rainbow' Garrett...Technical & Composition
Debbie Hines...Production Artist
Front & Back Cover Art...Marlene McCauley

Song of Kateri
Princess of the Eucharist
by *Marlene McCauley*

Editor: R. Allan McCauley

Grace House Publishing
6237 N. 15th St.
Phoenix, Arizona 85014

Other Works by Marlene McCauley

Adventures with a Saint, Kateri Tekakwitha, Lily of the Mohawks (1992), Grace House Pub.

Circus on Strings, (video production), Popcorn Puppet Playhouse, Grace House Pub.

Collection of Poetry, (philosophical, nature, whimsical)

Lily of the Mohawks, (children's puppet drama, video production), Grace House Pub.

Miracle of the Roses, (drama)

Our Lady of Fatima, (drama)

Our Lady of Garabandal, (puppet musical)

Pretzel Story, (history, custom, prayer, recipe), Grace House Pub.

Whitey from Heaven: A Wondrous Cat, (2002), Grace House Pub.

Inquiries to:
Grace House Publishing
6237 N. 15th Street
Phoenix, Arizona
(602) 265-9151

Gratitude

My sincere gratitude to those who offered considerable help, prayers and encouragement related to the producing of this book. Heartfelt appreciation to computer wizard Skip Peshak without whose tireless efforts this work would not have seen completion. To my little family at LaMadeleine's Restaurant in Phoenix: Isis, Andrea, "Frenchie" Robert and their wonderful staff whose constant solicitousness while I'd be writing until minutes before closing kept my spirits high until the last line of the book was written, at which time, they celebrated, providing me with a delicious glass of wine!

To Bishop Donald Pelotte, SSS, a "Blessed Sacrament" priest of the Diocese of Gallip, NM; To Father Timothy Conlon of Native American Ministries of the Phoenix Diocese; To Father Alphonsus Duran, M.J. (Founder of the Order of Miles Jesu). To Bishop Thomas J. Olmstead of the Diocese of Phoenix.

To the Vice-Postulators of Kateri's cause in the U.S. and Canada: Father John Paret, S.J. of Auriesville, NY and Father Jacques Bruyére, S.J., of Kahnawake, Canada; To Father Terrence Curley of St. Thomas Aquinas Church in Nahant, MA (where the stained glass window is of St. Isaac Jo ues with Indians) who has a special devotion to Blessèd Kateri which he promotes. (The Church is where Father J. Walter Stocklosa, in 1974 displayed my painting "Kateri's Children of the World," created at "40 steps.") Father Stocklosa to this day loves and promotes Kateri's sainthood; To Msgr Paul Lenz, Director of Black & Indian Missions in Washington, DC; To Sister Kateri Mitchell, a Mohawk, Executive Director of the Tekakwitha Conference; To Dr. Alice Von Hildebrand, a regular on EWTN, Philosopher, Author and Professor Emeritus of Hunter College; To Anne Scheuerman, loyal friend, Kateri promoter and photographer of Blessed Kateri events and Professor Emeritus of Monroe College;

To my staff of children artists, all "Friends of Kateri," including students and teachers from Ville de Marie Academy in Scottsdale and St. Maxmillian Kolbe School in Phoenix; To the California youth: Kateri Lemmon, Anna Van Hecke, our grandchildren, the Wood Family, (of the Celtic Spring Band), and the Tesoriero sisters, Paula & Hannah from Phoenix — a big THANKS!

Finally, I give thanks to God for my darling husband Allan, my eternal pal of forty-eight years at this date. He is a walking dictionary, an inveterate romanticist an incurable humorist, a defender of the faith and my most charming editor...always readily available during breaks from legal practice over a year's period to help edit *Song of Kateri...Princess of the Eucharist*.

Thank you – God Bless you.

Acknowledgements

May Blessed Kateri smile upon the following friends and family members who offered loving prayers and/or financial assistance. Masses will be offered for your generosity at the Shrine of the North American Martyrs where your intentions will be prayed for:

Fr. Girard Steckler, S.J.; Fr. Joseph Walen, LS; Sisters of St. Joseph; Magnificat Ministries; Kateri Tekakwitha CUF (Catholics United for Faith); Catholic Family Rosary; Miles Jesu Community; Our Lady of Grace Prayer Group; Schmitt Jewelers 35th; David & Joan Kelly family; John & Barbara Moran family; Diane Juke family; Arnold & Nancy Sodikoff family; Anne Scheuerman family; Mastrangelo family; Rev. J. Walter Stocklosa; Josephine Stocklosa; Catherine Sullivan family; Arthur & Jane Oldoni; Lottie O'Malley & extended family; Thomas More & Margaret McCauley; Mark, Emily, Nicolas and Joseph Embrey family; Embrey Godchildren; Bernie, Susan, Stephanie, Sasha Bujnak (Mark & Emily Embrey's friends); Special Intention for Barbara McElroy; Lillian Carr & family; Frank & Rosemary Giunuzzi (Special Intention); Shelly & Tim Letendre and Elizabeth, Amy & Anna Clare; Matt, Madison and Miles Mahowald; Lisa Mahowald, Matthew, Meghan & Mitchell; Gary & Sharon Swigart; Frank & Catherine Snyder & family; Pat McGinnis family; Thomas, Carmela and Chris Hughes; Robert Rodiziguez; Sr. Mary Carmel, OP; Sr. Conchita Carrillo; Frank & Natalie Shaw family; Gregory & Mary Wood family; Joseph & Jennifer McCauley family; Wayne & Martha Jones family; Bill Rice family; Paul Carman family; Darrell Burch family; Dr. Robert & Dorothy Westfall family; Tom & Pat McDonald family; Richard Rochford family; Dr. Robert & Marge Wood family; Lucy Dossett & family; Francis Xavier, Anna Teresa, Rory & Patrick McCauley; Peter McCauley; Rich & Rosemarie Fox family; Jan Stoffas's intentions; friend "Larry" Hilmert family; Fr. Joseph Fichtner, C.C.; Dr. Charles & Mary Ellis family; Kateri Shrine, Pawhusks, OK; Peter & Edna McCauley family, Robert & Teresa Degnan family; George & Eileen McCauley family; Jean McCauley & family, Michael Van Hecke family; BD & Liz Dautsch family; Bart & Brenda Tesoriero family; Kathy Tesoriero – Special Intention; Al & Joan Garman families; Mary Caddell and Peg Oursland; Chet Adams family; Catherine Wood family; Sophia Munson family; St Regis Mission, Akwesasne; St. Francis X. Mission, Kahnawake, Canada; Mary di Concini; Viola & Tillie Teitel family; Carol Constantino; Justin & Pat Sorrelman family; Ted & Grace Yund family; Tom Tighe family; Keith, Karen & Erin Boswell family; Jason & Dorothy Morley; Mike McCartney family; Dr. Dudley & Pat Halpe family; Fr. Thomas Reddimasu; Inez Nestor family; Ralph & Joan Stears; George & Ann Heilshorn; Jon Roberson; Lloyd & Linda Valente; Gretchen Heilshorn; Fr. Terrence Curley; St. Thomas Aquinas Church, Nahant, MA; Fr. Charles Onyango, S.J. (Intention); Tekakwitha Conference; Dr. Charles & Kay Dries family; Betsy Parker family; Mary Beth, Jaye and Jane; the Raines; Jordan family, Joseph Cavanaugh family; Rev. Walter M. Abbot, S.J.; Donaldson family; Fr. George Belgarde, S.J. (St. Regis); Albert & Eileen Lazarre family; To our Beloved Native Americans & families; Carmel Mary Brandeis; David & Cathy Harris family; Dr. Thomas & Teresa Mulligan family; Fr. Joseph Kenny (Fonda Shrine); Remi & Alma Ruiz; Marie McClumpha; Fr. Alvaro Alvarez (St. F. X. Mission); Frank McCaffrey; Joan Sweeney; Charlotte Provencher; Fern Carron; Joanne Kichton; Diego Paoletti

Kateri Tekakwitha
Born - Auriesville, N.Y.,
1656

Kateri Tekakwitha
Died in Kahnawake,
Canada, April 17, 1680

Marlene with her "Friends of Kateri:
children artists, Rosalie Simoneau, 10
& Teresa Hundelt, 8

In Tribute

A Tribute to the loved ones of
"Friends of kateri"
We have been a great inspriation to us on earth and
have since joined the Chruch Triumphant...We miss you!
Masses will be offered for the following souls at the Shrine
of the North American Mortyrs. The following list is only
a small cluster of the departed multitude:

Pope John Paul II – The Great {Saint-to-Be}
Sr. Lucia - Immaculate Heart of Mary
Maria Esperanza de Bianchini
Dr. Dietrich Von Hildebrand
Archbishop Edward J. McCarthy
Rev. Girard Lavigne, S.J.
All our beloved Kateri Priests
Rev. John Schug, O.F.M., cap.
Sr. Gail Singel, O.P.
Sr. Bon Seccour, O.P.
Sr. Basil, O.P.
Rev. Thomas Egan, S.J.
Relatives & friends of
Mark & Emily Embrey
Francis Dee Ford, Jr.
Dr. & Mrs. Vic Mulligan
R.J. and Alice Blas
Stephen "Red" O'Malley
Tom & Margo McCauley families
Bill & Nora McKiernan
John Brandeis
Harry & Margaret Stinson
Ted & Marian de Grazia
Arthur Huggard
George Juke
Jeff Mahowald
Lee & Clare Kieffer
Benjamin & Laura Monette
Peter & Janine Robaczewski
Anne Wrzos
Patrick Brett
Frank Knoell
Mary Callary
Eileen Catherine Curley
Rob & Ella Stears
Jim Carr

Gene McElroy
Matthew J. Connors
Mary M. Connors
Family members of Fr. J. Walter Stocklosa
Theodora Freida
Charles Cecil
John Kuewite
Vernon & Charlotte
Monatelati Smweker
Anna Collete
Andrew and Stella Comeau
John Aubes
John McCauley
Michael & Mary Ellen McCauley
"Jackie" Louise Lemmon
Cheryl Maynard
Tom Constantino
Catherine & Ames Duggan
Don Woolbright
Angel Althea Rose Shaw
Robert Munson
Helen Carman
John Hughes
Cecile Adams
Katherine Degnan
Alma Bailey
Alex, Lena & William "Buster" Mitchell
Cathy Harris family members
Opal Rector
Mahowald & Swigart families
O'Malley family members
Sr. Mary Roberta, SMR
Dr. & Mrs. John J. Griffin
Fr. Francis X. Weiser, S.J.
Mary Eunice Spagnola
Paul Murphy, Miles Jesu {Saint-to-Be}

"The church has declared to the world that Kateri Tekakwitha is blessed; that she lived a life on earth of exemplary holiness and that she is now a member in Heaven with the Communion of Saints who continually intercede with the merciful Father on our behalf...."

...spoken by Pope John Paul II addressing the faithful at the Beatification of Kateri Tekakwitha on June 22, 1980... Vatican City.

Dedication

Celebrating the 25th Anniversary of Kateri's Beatification and the 325th Anniversary of her death, April 17, 1680.

To our dearly beloved - the late.
Pope John Paul II...the Great
1920 - 2005

To his Holy Successor
Pope Benedict XVI
April - 2005

To my Saintly Mother "Laura"
To all our Native Americans
and other friends of Kateri

To my darling husband Allan,
our six children and thirteen grandchildren

United in the Sacred and Immaculate
Hearts of Jesus and Mary
And especially to our precious
Kateri Tekakwitha, "Lily of the Mohawks"

Foreword

Monsignor Paul A. Lenz
Executive Director
Bureau of Catholic Indian Missions
Washington, DC

Prior to 1980, Marlene McCauley had a great interest in the Indian maiden known as the "Lily of the Mohawks." Marlene developed an even greater love for Kateri on and following June 22, 1980, when the same young Indian woman, Kateri Tekakwitha was honored by the Catholic Church. On that date, our late Holy Father, Pope John Paul II at the Vatican proclaimed her Blessèd Kateri Tekakwitha. She became the first person with American blood to be so honored by the Church.

Marlene was present at the Mass at St. Peter's Basilica and was so moved that immediately, thereafter, she began to promote Blessèd Kateri by becoming a very important advocate for the next step to get the "Lily of the Mohawks" named Saint Kateri Tekakwitha.

By producing books, poems, essays and paintings and by promoting Kateri at World Youth Day in Toronto and lecturing all over the U.S. and conducting pilgrimages to shrines the world over, Marlene has given much of her life and her many talents to the cause of Blessèd Kateri.

I am delighted to recommend *Song of Kateri...Princess of the Eucharist*, Marlene's latest creation on Kateri's behalf.

This work is superbly executed and wonderfully innovative and will no doubt serve Kateri and her readers well along her and their path to sainthood.

Preface

Peter McCauley, 11 at Beatification 1980
"Next in line to see the Pope"

In the year of 1973, I was introduced to Kateri Tekakwitha by my Philosophy Professor (Emmanuel College, Boston, Mass.), the late Father Francis Xavier Weiser, a Jesuit priest. Father Weiser was a great scholar and had just completed a book on Kateri's life when he asked me to arrange lectures throughout Arizona to introduce the laity to this most interesting, incredibly virtuous Indian maiden who lived in the Mohawk valley of NY state some three hundred years previous.

It was at this time that Father learned of Peter's (age four) severe chronic hearing loss to which knowledge, he exclaimed, "We will pray to Kateri, who will never leave a prayer unanswered!"

Peter's hearing was cured instantly on Kateri's feast day, April 17, 1973 without the need for surgical intervention. Peter's hearing remains perfect to this very day.

This has been the basis for my thirty "plus" years of devotion to Kateri.

Left to Right: Pope John Paul II, Gregory, Mary and Baby Elizabeth
Wood, Anne, Marlene & Allan Joseph McCauley

Marlene nudges our Holy Father to Canonize Kateri because the Native
Americans need a Saint.

Castel Gandolfo, Rome, 1985

Top row: Anne, Francis Xavier, Allan
Bottom row: Peter, Marlene, Mary, Tom More

McCauley Family Theatre; "Lily of Mohawks"
 (Video Presented to Pope John Paul II 1985, Rome)

Table of Contents

PART I
Kateri's Birth to Early Childhood
Song of Kateri...

PART II
Teenage to Baptism

PART III
Village of Prayer

PART IV
Postlude

Kateri's Tree of Life

Mary Frances Gilsdorb, 10

Important Dates in Kateri's Life

1656 Tekakwitha is born in Ossernenon (today, Auriesville, NY)

1660 An epidemic of smallpox carries off her mother, her little brother, and probably her father. Her aunts and uncle adopt her.

1667 Three Jesuit missionaries visit her village of Ossernenon and spend three days there.

1670 Fr. Francis Boniface comes to live at the village.

1675 Fr. James de Lamberville is appointed as Fr. Boniface's successor.

1676 Kateri Tekakwitha is baptized by Fr. James de Lamberville.

1677 In October, Kateri escapes to the Mission of St. Francis Xavier on the St. Lawrence River near Montreal.

1677 Kateri makes her first Holy Communion on Christmas Day.

1678 On Easter Sunday, Kateri is admitted to the Confraternity of the Holy Family.

1679 Kateri takes the vow of perpetual virginity on March 25, feast of the Annunciation.

1680 Kateri Tekakwitha dies on April 17, Wednesday of Holy Week.

1680 Kateri appears to Fr. Chauchertière on Easter Monday.

1680 She also appears to her friend Marie Theresa Tegaiaguenta.

1681 On September 1, she appears a second time to Fr. Chauchetière.

1682 During March, the first novena made to Kateri results in the cure of an Indian woman.

1939 The Cause for the canonization of Kateri Tekakwitha is accepted by the Congregation of Rites.

1943 Pope Pius XII formally declares the virtues of Kateri heroic, thereby, giving her the title of "Venerable."

1980 Pope John Paul II beatifies Kateri Tekakwitha.

Kateri Tekakwitha

Kateri Lemmon, 15, Santa Paula, Califonria (one of 9 children) drew this image of Kateri, honoring her dearest mother, Jacquiline Louise Lemmon who died, March 2, 2005 to join her precious saintly, Kateri Tekakwitha in Heaven!

Song of Kateri...

Princess of the Eucharist

Part I

PROLOGUE

Song of Kateri
Princess of the Eucharist

'Tis a story-poem,
     An 'epic' one may say,
Of saintly Kateri,
     Angel of Charity
Her path to eternity.

Proportion long,
     Sing as song
A little each day,
     Recite as you may.
Progress as you pray,

Whatever decide,
     You'll take a ride,
Through exciting history,
     Of Iroquois Nation...and
Kateri's salvation.

May her life's story inspire,
     Share as desire,
To know and love her, you'll learn,
     Follow her journey, you'll earn,
          For Jesus Christ, you'll burn,
His Cross and Eucharist, you'll yearn,
          ...the first page please turn...

Turtle
by Elizabeth Wood age 9

Longhouse

CANTO I
The Turtle Castle
Longhouse Way

Come dear children for a visit here,
  You are our friends...do not fear,
From the Mohawk River, look up the hill,
  See our longhouse with fields to till.

We are the Mohawks of the "Turtle Clan,"
  Non-migrant people of Hiawatha's Peace Plan,
One of five nations...the fiercest we are,
  Our friends we love but foes we chase far!

For protection, our village is well fortified,
  Doubly palisaded...longhouse inside,
Stockades reach up to twelve feet high,
  Above is the fortress for scouts to spy.

There, weapons are stored secretly,
  Warriors ready to make enemy flee!
To learn of our clan...tis the reason,
  A beautiful moon...the planting season.

Climb up the slope...to our village we'll go,
  The longhouse way, you'll get to know,
Bark-covered lodge with arched dome,
  Our "Turtle Castle" is home sweet home!

Now we will enter the palisade gate,
  Year: sixteen-fifty-six...special date,
In the center you'll see the scaffold high,
  Where enemy captives are tortured and die.

"Sagon-skennon-gowa," peace be with you,
  Come into our longhouse for an inside view,
Our Iroquois castle...we are thankful,
  Plantations surround with vegetable.

People of the
Longhouse
Mary Francis Gilsdorb, 12

Welcome to our
Longhouse!
Joseph Duyer, 6

Enter through bearskin...this curtain door,
    Now we will trod on the earthen floor,
Families here in groups of four,
    Compartments for sleep...soon you'll learn more.

Sleeping mats of bear and elk hide,
    Sharing hearth...two families each side,
Above each fire is the roof's vent,
    Where sun enters and smoke is sent.

Teeming with life till the sun goes down,
    The "Turtle Castle" alive in morn,
Cooking, eating...chores to perform,
    The air is filled with merry song.

The mother, "Queen," within the wall,
    Rules her family, clan and all,
Crops and fields to women belong,
    Teaching children right from wrong.

In charge of the lodge, she does demand,
    Respect for each other and "Mother Earth" land,
The women and girls plant, then harvest the seed,
    They help with the cooking...the family they feed.

Boys are trained by their fathers to fight,
    Swiftly run and climb great height,
To fish and hunt with strength and will,
    Build huts and canoes with iron skill.

Braves and warriors born to be,
    Protect the clan...their destiny,
A chief elected to keep them free,
    Bound by the spirit of democracy.

"Mr. Turtle"
Joseph McCauley, 5

Meadow and Sunshine

Marlene as
Meadow-Flower
in Production of
*"Lily of the
Mohawk's"*

Sunshine in Cradleboard

CANTO II
A Princess is Born

Now dear children, young and old,
    From distant lands our hands do hold,
To hear a tale of moons ago,
    Of an Indian maiden this rhyme will flow.

Of the Eastern woodland she was born,
    America of a brand new dawn,
A little babe of redskin face,
    In the valley of the Mohawk race.

Ossernenon...then its name,
    Now Auriesville of national fame,
Where holy martyrs shed their blood,
    'Twas this soil sprung our lily bud.

Born midst birch, maple and pine,
    To her was given the name..."Sunshine,"
"Great Beaver," Chief of the Turtle Clan,
    Married "Meadow," Algonquin from Canada-land,

She, a Christian to the Great Spirit was true,
    The Virgin and Saints she loved and knew,
She shunned superstitions and torture too,
    Prayed privately...kind acts did she do!

He a non-Christian, many Gods he had,
    Cajoled evil spirits when they got mad,
Followed his dreams what they dictated,
    The missionary Blackrobes he hated

Orgies of victory...ritual fire,
    Aireskoi and Manitou he did aspire,
For crop failure and dread disease,
    These demons of evil he did appease.

'Twas sixteen-fifty-six...Sunshine was born,
    A bright beginning of a beautiful dawn,
The birds, beasts and water-fowl,
    Sang with the forest's little hoot-owl!

Both were ecstatic at Sunshine's birth,
    The Chief made a vow to Mother Earth,
"NO BAPTISM FOR MY BABY DAUGHTER!!"
    Meadow still prayed for the holy water.

Meadow Flower's
Friend Anastasia
blesses the New
Princess
Sunshine

Sunshine...born a Princess at birth,
    Her funny antics brought them great mirth,
Deep inside, Meadow's heart was blue,
    Her prayer would be granted one day, she knew!

The Chief, a good husband, he so loved his wife,
    His clan and his tribe, he protected from strife,
A hero in battle...tough on the trail,
    To his family so gentle...he was without fail.

Meadow loved her Princess babe,
    Thankful for this gift God gave,
She cuddled and hugged her babe so dear,
    With joy sublime she shed a tear.

Into the longhouse entered a friend,
    Anastasia, a Christian, loyal to end,
She congratulated Meadow...all aglow,
    Kissed baby Sunshine from head to toe.

"Please Anastasia," Meadow did plea,
    Pray for my babe that baptized she'll be,
Great Beaver would never let the Blackrobe here,"
    Anastasia replied, "With God, have no fear!"

She traced a cross on Sunshine's brow,
    To her friend Meadow, "I must go now,"
Meadow prepared to take a walk,
    To give her babe a cradleboard rock.

In deerskin soft, her babe did she wrap,
    Into carved cradleboard onto her back,
A walk through the woods, the two did go,
    To the squirrels and chipmunks, a cheery, "Hello!"

Meadow hung papoose on a branch low,
    Sunshine swayed as soft wind did blow,
The birds in the trees burst with song,
    As Meadow picked corn near her firstborn!

While her basket was filling during this time,

    She sang a song for her babe Sunshine.

    "Swing high, swing low,
      While wind doth blow,
And bluebirds fly so high,
    The sun is out, the sky is blue,
What a wonderful thing to do!"

When Sunshine was two, a brother was born,
    Sugar, his name...sweet as corn,
Together they played from sun's rise to its set,
    A happy boy, he did not whimper nor fret.

His children asleep on the skins of bear,
    Great Beaver pondered his precious pair,
"One day my child a brave she'll wed,
    We'll choose the mightiest one," he said.

"Our custom sanctions the marriage seal,
    When the bride feeds the groom...sagamité meal,
We will witness this event so grand,
    Her spouse will help me in Mohawk land."

"Oh God of the upper world, fulfill this dream,
    Keep Manitou and Aireskoi from our team,
Let my son be courageous and strong."
    He prayed to Great Spirit early one morn.

Meadow with Sunshine and Sugar   *Amy Toman, 8*

Princess Sunshine
by Hannah Tesoriero, 8

Child of Three
by Dierdre Wood, 7

"A Child of Three"

Sunshine, the name...her smile the same.
      When she was a child of three.
Deerskin tunic she wore and leggings more,
      When she was a child of three,
Moccasins of hide with beads outside,
      When she was a child of three,
Through the forest she ran...of the Turtle
clan,
      When she was a child of three,
Black braids hung long...she sang a song.
      "I AM A CHILD OF THREE!"

37

CANTO III
Mother Earth's Toys

Sunshine burst with great delight,
     When she saw a crocus white,
Peek its head through Mother Earth,
     Of spring's first flower, she sang with mirth.

Flower to flower, the humming bird flew,
     Sparkled and flashed its brilliant hue,
Wearing its most colorful gown,
     Sunshine chuckled, Great Spirit's Clown!

Once a tiny robin redbreast,
     Fell from a golden maple nest,
Many tears did Sunshine shed,
     Thinking that the bird was dead.

Glad to see it still alive,
     "DON'T YOU EVER TAKE A DIVE!"
She had her daddy place it back,
     With its mommy in the pack.

When a rainbow spanned the sky,
     Sunshine wished that she could fly,
To touch the sky's tremendous toy,
     Her soul in rapture with pure joy!

Through fragrant fields, Sunshine went seeking,
     Scampering bunnies...always leaping,
Little white phantoms in starlit night,
     Her happy heart jumped at the sight!

Sunshine loved the birds that sing,
     Perfumed fragrance flowers bring,
Music of the river flowing,
     Lacy leaves and soft winds blowing.

Squirrels staring with big black eyes,
     Ladybugs and butterflies,
A turtle crawling through moss of green,
     Sunshine's playland...Mother Earth's scene.

In wintertime when snowflakes fell,
     A glorious design, each one did tell,
Of creation...Great Spirit's powers,
     Sunshine compared them to little field flowers.

Far across the western sky,
     Sunshine gazed with sparkling eye,
At dazzling colors so sublime,
     By angel brush at sunset time.

When nature drew its darkened veil,
     Stars in the Heavens she would hail,
Wreathed with diamonds in the sky,
     Sunshine's soul was lifted high.

A babe of the woods...creation, her love,
     Grateful to Great Spirit above,
As a flower unfolds in the moon of spring
     Sunshine grew under Mother Earth's wing!

Kateri and Turtle

CANTO IV
How Mother Earth Came To Be
Iroquois Mythology

Sunshine and Great Beaver were out for a walk,
    "Father," she blurted, "STOP, STOP!"
She picked up the creature from the mossy dale,
    The tortoise chief told a tall turtle tale!

The Chief of the Ancients, a spouse he took,
    Ambitious she was with lovcly look,
But jealous he was which made him sick,
    The Medicine man had a cure with a trick.

"'Uproot the tree of light,' he said,
    Into the hole have her put her head,
Push her gently...she'll fall into space,
    Through a long tunnel, she will race!"

Sunshine hears a Turtle Tale

She found herself under the sky,
     Through an open space, she did fly,
A duck looked up from water below,
     Quacked the quackiest "quack quack HELLO!"

A meeting was called and plans were made,
     Of all water fowl to come to her aid,
The turtle gave his back as a field to land,
     The muskrat dove for mud and sand.

Mud on the turtle would make a soft bed,
     For the girl-being to land without hurting her head,
Poor muskrat died...water-fowl did toil,
     From their mouths took the mud to the dry soil.

Spreading their wings, caught the girl in mid-air,
     Placed her on turtle's back with care,
By magic of Ancients, the tortoise did grow,
     In all directions, the firm land did flow.

The turtle grew huge with sand on its surf,
     In the midst of this water came great "Mother Earth."
This turtle tale tells how the earth came to be
     "Now my Sunshine, let your little friend flee!"

"Maples"

In the moons of spring, summer, winter and
fall,
     Queen of the trees, the maple stood tall,
In robes of green, orange or white,
     Whatever the season...a sensational
sight!

Nativity

©Marlene McCauley

CANTO V
Sunshine's Christmas

One Christmas morn...forest white,
    Snowflakes fell...a wonder bright,
Bitter cold...the longhouse wall,
    Sunshine hugged her cornhusk doll.

Great Beaver away on the winter hunt,
    With arrows and traps for the brutal stunt,
The spoils of the chase for his family of four,
    Fur skins to scrape...much game to store.

Anastasia, by the glowing fire squat,
    Helping to keep the embers hot,
This day, baby Sugar was in her care,
    For Meadow and Sunshine...a time rare.

Soon ready for their jaunt in the morn,
    Fur skins, leggings and boots so warm,
Gloves and caps to shield from cold,
    The two were dressed for the weather bold.

Snowshoes they took from the sapling beam,
    Mother and child, a brave rugged team,
Meadow's burden strap fastened so,
    To search for wood, the two did go.

Thunder, their dog barked with might,
    To go with them must be his plight,
To guard the team would be his job,
    Meadow and Sunshine invited their dog.

Sunshine & Thunder leave for home.

The north wind blew...trees cracked with cold,
      Two figures at times...their hands did hold,
As the wild wind whistled, they trudged along,
      Meadow was inspired to sing a song.

"My darling child, a carol I'll sing,
      I learned as a child of the *Infant King*,
'Twas written by *Brebeuf,* for the Indian child,
      This holy Blackrobe...meek and mild."

The wind calm...silence fell,
      Of the *Christ Child,* Meadow did tell,
A scarlet bird on a snow-clad tree,
      Iesos A-ha-ton-hia,...its melody.

Though Meadow's child was only three,
      She struggled to sing with happy glee,
As they trod the morning long,
      She sang, *"Jesus is born! Jesus is born!"*

The two staggered in untracked snow,
      Thunder, ever watchful of woodland foe,
Sunshine would pause at each little tread,
      "Mama," she cried, "You're too far ahead!"

Once the wind beat her down in the snow,
      Rising, laughing, to her mother did go,
Thunder followed as they descended the slope,
      To the ravine was their hope.

Deep into the snow, their hands did go,
      Plucking sticks from surface below,
Thunder dug deep...gave a big yelp,
      Happy to find wood, he was a big help!

Out of its mouth into her pack,
      Heavy the strain of her burden strap,
Meadow brushed snow from a wooden beam,
      Thunder slid dizzily on the frozen stream.

Meadow's mind began to dream,
      Amidst this wondrous winter scene,
Sunshine listened as her mother did tell,
      Of a Blackrobe's plight...for *Jesus* he fell.

Of *Isaac Jogues* and his *Jesus Tree*
      How Jesus died for you and me.
"*Jogues* carved a cross on his *Jesus Tree,*
      Jesus died to set man free."

When Meadow explained the *Jesus Tree,*
      Sunshine's heart danced with glee,
"A *Jesus Tree* I want to find,"
      Only three years she knew her mind.

One last word before they depart,
      Mother to daughter from her heart,
"When the maple unveils her gown so white,
      We'll find a *Jesus Tree*...in sight."

On a snow-clad tree, she traced a cross,
      The word Jesus she did endorse,
Meadow to Sunshine exclaimed, "SEE!"
      "We made our own white *Jesus Tree!*

This Christmas morn...a brand new song,
      Jesus is born...Jesus is born,
Curiosity stirred the Princess soul
      To learn of the *Blackrobe* and his holy role.

Meadow gave Sunshine a loving kiss,
      'Twas a memorable white Christmas.
Thunder's tail wagged when Meadow did smile,
      "TIME TO LEAVE WITH OUR WOODPILE!"

Francis Xavier, Thomas More, Peter McCauley
McCauley Family Production "Lily of the Mohawks"

CANTO VI
Blackrobes

"*Blackrobes* my dear are holy men,
     Who bring Christ's love to God's children,
They don black robes and broad-brimmed hats,
     Carry supplies in rugged backpacks,
The *Bible,* their beads and *Holy Mass* things,
     Love in their heart and a spirit that sings.
Their call as Jesuits...to save each soul,
     Christ's gospel is their priestly goal,
From New France they came to our strange land,
     Some captured by the Mohawk band,
Brutally beaten, dragged down the trail,
     Prayed for the tormentors...their souls not to fail.
For preaching God's word, by the tomahawk fell,
     Father Isaac Jogues and his helper *Goupil.*
John La Lande and many more,
     For *Jesus Christ,* their love did soar.
For His love, *Goupil's* blood was shed,
     For tracing a cross on a little boy's head.
For a crop failure...*Jogues* blamed for the blight,
     His Mass kit they said was an evil sight,
One blow with the axe, he was in God's light.
     Jogues called *Ondessonk...Bird of Prey,*
Put into captivity a year and a day,
     Sixteen-forty-two to sixteen-forty-three,
'Twas the time he carved the *Jesus Tree.*
     This woodland, his chapel midst maple and birch,
He prayed the Aves in his green forest church,
     The cross he did carve with *Jesus'* name,
Before this tree, his heart aflame!
     As he knelt before the *Jesus Tree,*
He felt Christ's loving mercy.
     Once dear Ondessonk had a dream,

He saw a gold city surround the ravine,
    A prophetic dream...*God* did assign,
Today it is...a holy shrine.
    A *Christian* I am because of *Jogue's* blood,
Algonquins saved by his acts of love.
    Ondessonk, Ondessonk, your spirit is here,
Your anointed body is hiding near,
    Please wash my little one with your blood,
So that she will be *God's lily* bud."
    They said a prayer and kissed goodnight,
Grateful that the day was bright;
    "Thank you mommy for telling me,
Of the *Blackrobes* plight and the *Jesus Tree!*"

The Jesus Tree — Isaac Jogues

CANTO VII
The Jesus Tree

Great Beaver took Sugar for a canoe ride,
      While Meadow and Sunshine walked outside,
'Twas the moon of flowers...colorful scene,
      To search for a *Jesus Tree* was their dream!

A song to *Great Spirit* as they did look
      While searching every cranny and nook,
"Please help us find the *Jesus Tree*
      Only *You* know where it be!"

Midst brambles and bush, the two did seek,
      A holy carved tree by the bubbling creek,
Hopping o're rocks, they had great fun,
      Rustling midst leaves, a song they sung.

"The Jesus Tree, the Jesus Tree
      Ondessonk did so love Thee,
He carved a cross on a maple tree,
      For Jesus Who died at Calvary."

The sun was sinking in the west,
      They'd return again for quest,
Sunshine saw Meadow carve on a tree,
      Jesus and a *Cross*, so lovingly.

"Always remember this lesson I give,
      The *Cross of Jesus* is for what you must live,
He shed His blood for you and me,
      His love did flow from the *Jesus Tree!"*

When Mr. Moon cast its yellow glow,
      The Princess fading, her thoughts did flow,
"*Jesus* so loved you and me,
      He died on the cross at Calvary."

Shaman

CANTO VIII
Smallpox

Sadness fell one winter moon,
    Ossernenon filled with gloom,
Smallpox plague like fire spread,
    Sixteen fifty-nine...tears shed.

Groaning, moaning, shrieking, wailing,
    Warriors, braves...families failing,
Burning fever racked with pain,
    The dying fell like falling rain.

The dread disease caused lamentation,
    Ravaging the Iroquois nation,
Like a lion devouring its prey,
    Turtle clan dwindling night and day.

False Face Masks

Frantic figures round fire leaping,
    Haunting rattles...drums beating,
Masked faces...colors streaking,
    To appease the "Okis," they were seeking!

The God of evil..."Manitou,"
    "Aireskoi" of war, were but a few,
Demons of sick could not be swayed,
    To stop the deadly dismal plague.

The Mohawk castle in grim despair.
    Choking fumes filled the air,
Shamans and sorcerers could not heal,
    Their herbs and charms...hopeless deal.

59

Ritual drums beat dismal din,
        Dead carried to forest rim,
Once alive, fierce and brave,
        Now buried in shallow grave.

A mournful tale 'tis time to tell,
        Of how a cross on a child's heart fell,
The village resounded with tear-filled grief,
        Upon the death of Great Beaver..."Chief!"

False Face
Masks

Amongst Turtle Clan, the word spread,
        "Tsa-niton-gowa is DEAD...DEAD!"
A mysterious spell filled the air,
        The demon of death...they were aware!

Shaken by spasms of the fever hot,
        Tossing on mat, the sickness fought,
Meadow and children evoked a loud cry,
        "Great Beaver our love, Good bye, Good bye!"

Under heap of pine, Thunder howled,
        His master died by smallpox fouled,
As he lay on the stretcher clothed in hide,
        The dog lapped his face and curled by his side.

Amidst whimpering cries of his family,
        Taken with moccasins for his journey,
Face oiled...hair stiff in a ridge,
        His spirit took flight to the upper-world bridge.

As Meadow lay suffering in great agony,
        She dreamed of Jogues and his Jesus Tree,
How Christ shed His blood for earth's family,
        That man may live eternally.

To Jesus, she prayed in thanksgiving,
        "Take Great Beaver to your land of living,
Save his soul that we may be,
        With each other in eternity."

Death of Great Beaver

Gone was his body...her husband, the Chief,
     Tears spilled from her eyes...her heart at peace.
She caressed baby Sugar under her arm,
     "Bless he and Sunshine...keep them from harm,"
Meadow-flower wilting...on death's bed she lay
     Anastasia beside her, knelt to pray,
"My friend," Meadow whispered, faint and weak,
     "One day in Heaven, we all will meet."

"Guide my children in Christian love,
     That they will be led to God above,"
Her color fading as she lifted her head,
     Jesus, have mercy on me, she said.

Iesos-tak-won-tonr," the prayer,
Softly, she gazed toward Heaven fair,
Kahontake's head sank on the arm of her friend,
Anastasia knew this was the end.

Her face had a smile ...all gone was strife,
Meadow-flower blossomed to eternal life,
As her mother lay lifeless and limp on her mat,
Sunshine gave her a loving pat.

The child by her mother...heartrending scene,
"Great Spirit, please bless this tender team!"
Anastasia embraced her as she cried and cried,
Another cross same day...her brother had died!

Meadow Dies   *Sam Jukubcyzk, 8*

Anastasia Cares for Sunshine

CANTO IX
Sunshine's Struggle Between Life and Death

Sunshine lay listless on Anastasia's lap,
  With sad heart, the aunt saw future black,
The child's life at stake...she could die anytime,
  If she lived, she'd suffer in tender prime.

Ten days Sunshine shook with sickness that tore,
  Her face scarred with the smallpox sore,
With Anastasia's care, each day without ceasing,
  The ugly disease was at last releasing.

Recovery slow...Sunshine weak,
  "Soon you'll fly with swift little feet!"
Anastasia tried with kind words to console,
  Her heart broken to see Sunshine's sad soul.

Apparent effects from battling blight,
  Sunshine turned from chimney-hole light,
"I cannot see you," she cried in fright,
  Anastasia knew her eyes not right.

With vision dim, she woke that morn,
  The harvest scanty... family gone,
On withering stalks, corn heavily hung,
  Sunshine in darkness...cross begun.

Her silken beauty, pox did erase,
  Pock-pitted was ...Sunshine's face,
Feebly she groped with her cornhusk doll,
  Her aunt held her hand so she would not fall.

To Anastasia, her heart did grieve,
     "Why, auntie, did my family leave?"
From Rawennio, an answer she found,
     "He took them to Happy Hunt Ground!"

The little girl asked when would she die,
     "I want to be with mommy," her sigh,
Anastasia hugged and gave her a kiss,
     "One day you'll meet in eternal bliss!"

While Sunshine sat so silent and still,
     Her aunt spoke of the Great Spirit's Will,
"Obedient to Him...we must always be,"
     Sunshine thought of the cross on the Jesus Tree!

Sunshine asleep on her deerskin mat,
     Her aunt said a prayer then a kiss and pat,
Thunder, the dog, beside his friend sat,
     Wagging his tail, while her face he did lap!

Puppets: Anastasia consoles Sunshine   *from McCauley Puppet Theatre*

"A Child of Four"

Sunshine, the name,
      Her smile NOT the same,
When she was a child of four,
      She was sad inside,
And wanted to hide,
      When she was a child of four
Her family gone,
      She did not belong,
When she was a child of four,
      She lost some of her sight,
Her face pitted by blight,
      When she was a child of four,
An orphan was she,
      She lost all her glee,
When she was a child of four.
      A cross at her door,
And more in store,   "I AM A CHILD OF FOUR!"

A Child of Four
by Paula Tesoriero, 11

67

Cold Wind, Adoptive Unclc

CANTO X
Transition

Anastasia bid Sunshine farewell,
      Tearfully they did embrace,
The future years she knew would tell,
      Meadow's prayers would shower grace.

When 'ere a blight or smallpox struck,
      The clan would then move on,
Blamed gods of evil for bad luck,
      But soon a bright new dawn.

To Ganawagé from Ossernenon
      Where rapid waters flow,
Uprooting clan...painful song,
      Sunshine's spirit low.

Sunshine, a little child of four,
      Indeed a strange transition,
Another cross for her in store,
      New parents for submission.

Her twinkling eyes began to stare,
      Pockmarks mapped her face,
Vision dimmed by sun's bright glare,
      New family to embrace.

Life's curtain drew this anguished scene,
      Sunshine's head hung low,
Felt alone...painful dream,
      Gone...her healthy glow.

Enita

Elizabeth Wood, 9

Cold Wind, uncle, became her dad,
      Cook, his wife...her mother
Squirrel, aunt...to these we add,
      Orphaned Enita another.

Enita, thirteen, a servant child,
      They worked her to the bone,
A sweet nature, meek and mild,
      All day she toiled for home.

Sunshine's spirit fled all day,
      With her mother blending,
The one she loved with her would stay,
      Love signals...Meadow sending.

"Happy Hunting Ground"...Heaven,
      Where her mother dwells,
Sunshine's heart filled with leaven,
      When heard the angel bells.

As moons sped by, Sunshine became,
      Accepting of her life,
Joy within her heart did reign,
      Her smile erased all strife.

The Turtle Chief though proud he be,
      Warlike, heart of stone,
Behind his mask, Sunshine did see,
      A loving warming tone.

Her uncle's heart began to melt,
      When Sunshine stretched her hands,
To lead her way by things she felt,
      Her weak eyes made demands.

Blind to things within her range,
      She bumped and stumbled so,
Time for her name to change,
      "HER BABY NAME MUST GO!"

He knew her vision somewhat blurred,
    Her steps...hesitated,
TEKAKWITHA...he concurred,
    When 'ere...he meditated.

The name in Mohawk signifies,
    "Feeling all the way,"
Making order as she tries,
    "THIS...HER NAME WILL STAY!"

Tekakwitha and Doll   *Elizabeth Wood, 9*

"A Child of Eight"

"Tekakwitha" new name...the chief did deign,
     When she was a child of eight,
"Feeling one's way"...the name will stay,
     When she was a child of eight.
Hazy sight...her plight...pockmarks from blight,
     When she was a child of eight,
Frail and shy...she did not sigh,
     When she was a child of eight.
Red shawl she wore...from field to door,
     When she was a child of eight.
Protection from light...the sun too bright,
     When she was a child of eight.
An artist was she...created with glee,
     When she was a child of eight.
All day she worked...she never shirked
     When she was a child of eight.
Betrothed to a mate...the custom to take,
     "I AM A CHILD OF EIGHT!"

A Child of Eight
by Nathan, age 9

Tekakwitha brings water from the spring   *Elizabeth, 9*

CANTO XI
Busy Like a Bee

A child of eight...though frail and shy,
    Kept by herself but never did sigh,
Did all her chores when they were given,
    Seeking perfection, she was driven.

She collected dry wood...an extra supply,
    Entrance of cabin, she stacked it high,
Fetched water at the spring in a kettle,
    Willing to help even when about to settle.

With pestle of wood crushed kernels of maize,
    Gathered berries and mushrooms other days,
Cooked cornmeal the base for the Iroquois fare,
    Prepared maple syrup, the best in her care.

Squatting on earth next to her bed,
    Fingers nimble, sewed bands for the head,
Of dried skins of eel in green, blue or red,
    Designs..."superb," everyone said.

Tekakwitha wove cornhusks into mats,
    She learned to make cords of bast,
Animal skins sewn with tendons fine,
    Of elk or deer, her work did shine.

Fringes of flat porcupine quills,
    She used for dress, leggings and frills,
Wampum beads and river shells,
    Small ringlets for necklace bells.

Betrothal at Eight

Tekakwitha's aunts kept her busy with work,
　　　　The child of eight never once did shirk,
The Turtle Chief loved his gifted daughter,
　　　　She grasped quickly what 'ere was taught her.

Sitting by fire, her uncle thought,
　　　　While he blew circles of smoke from his calumet,
"Tekakwitha, one day, a brave she will marry,
　　　　My tribe's burdens, he'll help to carry."

"Now we'll betroth her to a boy her age,
　　　　An Iroquois custom for the young to engage,
Not meant to be a permanent bond,
　　　　But strengthens the tie with a family we're fond."

Neither boy nor girl did this marriage impress,
　　　　In finest array Tekakwitha did dress,
With painted face and sparkling beads,
　　　　Pierced ears with rings of colored seeds.

Feasting, dancing...much elation,
　　　　For the grandest celebration,
Though against her inclination,
　　　　Tekakwitha hid vexation.

The little girl...child of eight,
　　　　Donned in deerskin wedding dress,
Wore beads and buckskins for the date,
　　　　Who would be her future mate?

Fishing Trip — Enita and Kateri Fishing

Patrick Wood, 12

CANTO XII
Fishing Trip

"Pack up your gear for a fishing trip week,"
    The Turtle Chief's voice resounded deep,
"We'll canoe down the Mohawk to the Hudson today,
    To the Holandish colony of Fort Oranje."

"The Iroquois are on friendly terms,
    With Dutch settlers, have no concerns,
Firearms, firewater, they give us galore,
    In trade for our furs, deerskins and more."

Tekakwitha and Enita flowing with joy,
    Fishing for them...the greatest toy,
Step-sisters they are...each lost her mother,
    Love filled their hearts for one another.

They gathered all gear...enough for five days,
    The family would camp near the cascades,
Tawas?nta, 'twas called near the tumbling-down river,
    They packed beaver and moose skins so not to shiver.

Canoeing was fun, o'er boat she would kneel,
    Tekakwitha bent over...the water to feel,
Ripples she made as her fingers would glide,
    From Mohawk to Hudson adventuresome ride.

Fascination betook her on the Hudson shore,
    At the houses of wood with chimney and door,
Tekakwitha stared with wonder and glee,
    Nothing like this did she ever see!

Palace of wood...the paleface home,
      Two stories high...no longhoused dome,
Soon the roar of the river was heard,
      Too loud to hear the song of the bird.

Of branches pine their huts were made,
      Topped with moose skins in the shade,
Beaver pelts on earthen ground,
      The girls, dry wood for the fire found.

Cozy wigwams sheltered from rain,
      Uncle and aunts to Towas?nta came,
For salmon, trout, perch and eels,
      They would catch for many meals.

To the river they hiked with fishing supplies,
      Prepared to return with the prize,
With nets and angles below waterfall,
      Three hundred pounds was their haul.

They cut and cleaned the fish with zest,
      Never stopping for a rest,
On rocks and wood o'er logs a glowing,
      Smoked the fish so over flowing!

Dried fish packed in baskets brought,
      This art from generations taught,
By fire, the family gathered round,
      For all their labor great food found.

Cornbread, trout and beans, the meal,
      Smoldering fire...succulent eel,
The Chief near fire did squat with pipe,
      The aunts chatted in starlit night.

Tekakwitha and Enita on a rock sat,
        At the rim of the river on a spot flat,
Dangling in water were their little feet,
        Filled with joy on this retreat.

Fragrance of pine...beauty of night,
        Reflection on Hudson's gold moonlight,
Spirits high...memorable fest.
        Day done...time to rest.

Laden with fish...heavy canoe,
        To Ganawagé...so much to do,
From summer to harvest...great fish supply,
        The work and fun did satisfy.

Memories   *Robert Rowland, 7*

CANTO XIII
Memories

'Twas a day in summer time,
    The Princess child of ten,
With little dog and cornhusk doll,
    Sat in a garden,
When memories of her mother dear,
    Flowered like a dream,
Transformed her to those days of ore,
    The two a loving team.

When once they trudged the winter scene,
    When she was only three,
Amidst the snow and ice-bound stream,
    She learned of the "*Jesus Tree.*"
Isaac Jogues called "Ondessonk,"
    A *Blackrobe* in exile,
Through torture and pain for Christ,
    He kept a glowing smile.

Her mother told her precious girl,
    A lesson Jogues had taught,
Christ shed blood for the world,
    His gospel must be wrought.
Jogues from France brought **Christ's love,**
    Among the Mohawk race,
In the forest of the trees,
    JESUS, he did trace.

The memory of that special day,
    Will forever linger on,
The lesson of her childhood...PRAY,
    Was life's anointed song,
A martyr for *Christ,* Jogues did toil,
    The cross he did embrace,
His blood did spill upon the soil,
    He met *God* face to face.

Memories

Mary O'Connor, 7

Tekakwitha...child of ten,
 Midst meadow-flowers dreamed,
Of her mother in Heaven
 As flashing lights beamed,
Drawn as a magnet to a tree,
 She took a sharp-edged stone,
A prayer of love she offered Thee,
 Carved a cross...then home.

The Jesus Tree...the Jesus Tree,
 Ondessonk did so love Thee.
Christ shed His blood for you and me,
 His love did flow from the Jesus Tree!

As Tekakwitha treked along,
 Sang the verse of her mother's song,
Of Christ's love for you and me.
 With dog and doll through brush they went,
Inhaling fragrance...wild flower scent.

Huron Wampum

CANTO XIV
Historical Background of French and Iroquois
Failure of the Great Plan

Come dear children, listen to me,
      To learn early American history,
At the close of the sixteenth century,
      Iroquois were bound by unity.

Hiawatha's peace plan for the five nations,
      Wise he was with steadfast patience,
A constitution set the foundation,
      Through upper New York...a new federation.

Senecas, Oneidas, Cayugas three,
      Onondagas, Mohawks all held the key,
Peace was theirs 'til conflict began,
      The tie broken when failed the great plan.

Tension arose 'tis sad but true,
      Hurons refused to join the league too,
Invitation by Iroquois to them given,
      Pride in their power caused rebellion.

Forty thousand to the five nation's twenty-six,
      "With Iroquois, we could not mix,"
The ground was dug for a dangerous bed,
      Armed jealousy loomed ahead.

In Quebec, the French settled...sixteen-ten,
      Traded in furs with Huron men,
To Iroquois...Hurons were unkind,
      For this, suffering their tribe would find.

So French with Iroquois would not compete,
     Slander by Hurons, vicious and bleak,
Rendered 'til the French believed,
     Innocent...they were deceived.

The great French Governor Champlain,
     A military trek south he came,
To attack the Iroquois in manner brutal,
     For Champlain, this move proved futile.

Enemies they were from that day on,
     Bitter to Hurons who caused the wrong,
Revenge on them they would dare,
     With guns from Dutch, they did prepare.

Tree of Peace

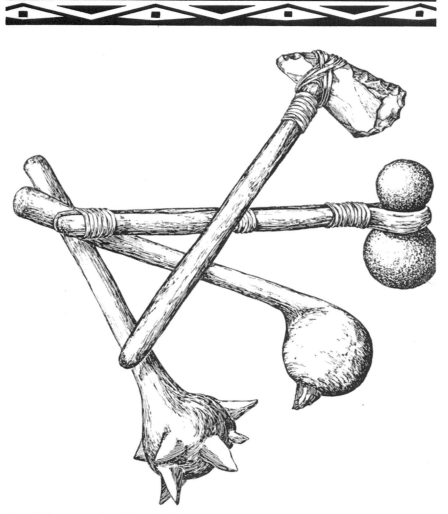

Warclubs, Tomahawk, Hatchet

CANTO XV
1648: War of Revenge

Friends with the French, the Hurons were true,
    Trading in furs, they continued to do,
Example of love the Jesuits gave,
    To be Christians like them, a new path to pave.

The Hurons welcomed the Blackrobes in,
    To learn the difference between good and sin,
Soon became Christians sincere,
    Eternal life to them was dear.

Peaceful they were farming their land,
    Happily content in God's loving hand,
The saddest tale I'm about to tell,
    The sun lost its shine...darkness fell.

'Twas the year sixteen-forty-eight,
    Revenge by Iroquois...their fate,
Hurons blamed for attack of Champlain,
    Through forest the Iroquois bands came.

'Twas the mid of winter in frosted cold,
    Their settlements raided by Iroquois bold,
Armed with rifles and rage they appeared,
    Hurons...no weapons...enemy they feared.

The Iroquios attacked with all their might,
    Thousands of Hurons died in fight,
Their farms and homes were destroyed
    Those remained...escape employed.

René Goupil, Isaac Jogues, John la Lande

Some fled to the Great Lakes domain,
      Pursued by Iroquois again and again,
Men, women and children captured in mass,
      Slaves they became for brutal harass.

Twelve Jesuit Blackrobes tortured for kill,
      Three in Ossernenon, now Auriesville,
Jogues among priests and donnés who died,
      North American Martyrs, the Church's pride.

The blood of the martyrs is the Church seed,
      By dying for Christ, new souls did they feed,
A lesson was given for you and for me,
      Christ died on the Cross to set man free.

By sixteen-forty-nine, the Hurons were done,
      But thereafter, Iroquois attack had become,
Incessant and constant with ferocious raids,
      They fought in Canada with arms and blades.

Four Iroquois tribes voted for peace,
      Their torture and terror to the French did cease,
All but the Mohawks, the fiercest race,
      Christian faith they despised of the French paleface.

With vigor and hatred they entered French land,
      Burning and looting with insidious hand,
Capturing and killing men by the score,
      Blood did spill with their war hoops and roar!

Peace   *Stephanie Young, 15*

CANTO XVI
French and Mohawks: 1666

The time came at last, the French yelled, "NO MORE!"
 A stand we'll take," spoke Governor,
Courcelles stood firm, "The Mohawks we'll fix!"
 The storm erupted, "Sixteen-sixty-six."

Great mountain of strength was the Marquis,
 De Tracy, General of the King's army,
In scarlet coat and tricorn hat,
 From massive head flowed wig so black.

French, Hurons and Algonquins too,
 Twelve hundred men with canons few,
Southward they moved toward Mohawk land,
 United the regiment...DeTracy's band.

The Mohawks learned their hour had come,
 For all the fighting they had done,
On New France soil much blood was shed,
 Those French tortured now lay dead.

Swiftly through forest ran the Mohawk,
 Clandestine and crafty, fast as a fox,
Returning with news a shock to reveal,
 The French revenge hit like steel!

The trees in crimson, red and gold,
 In stillness stood...a silence told,
A menacing black cloud was descending,
 Colossal plan...strategy blending.

The pumpkin downcast this harvest time,
　　　Squatted mournfully midst prickly vine,
An ominous cloud cast a gloomy spell,
　　　A pending battle, the air did tell.

The beans trembled, the corn turned white,
　　　Tekakwitha's heart fluttered with fright,
She was ten years old, will n'er forget,
　　　Turmoil midst strife her tribe met.

Soldiers advanced on weary feet,
　　　As throbbing drums in rhythm beat,
Air filled with victor's song,
　　　To see at last a glorious morn.

Though weary bones on mud did rest,
　　　And beds of dampened leaves,
They plodded on with hopeful zest,
　　　Through twisting paths of trees.

Tekakwitha, child of ten,
　　　Clad in bright red shawl,
Fright-filled midst mad mayhem,
　　　Clung to her cornhusk doll.

Stumbling o're stumps and roots,
　　　She fled with aunts in haste,
Thunder sped from howls and hoots,
　　　There was no time to waste.

The Chief from platform saw the view,
　　　As the French drew near,
His musket fell...he took the cue,
　　　Drums splitting to his ear.

Swiftly like a fox in flight
　　　Joined the wild stampede,
Stockade stark...a blackened night,
　　　The warrior's pride did bleed.

Arrows flashed and canons shot,
    As bullets whistled by,
French did torch the Turtle lot,
    Stripping food supply.

Mohawk land in devastation,
    As ashes covered ground,
The clan was left in desolation,
    But not a dead man found!

Village empty...families fled,
    From their tribal land,
To settle anew, they looked ahead,
    To give a helping hand.

Midst deadened trees, a cross was fixed,
    Deep into the ground,
The darkened air with light was mixed,
    Alas! God's love was found!

The warring French from Canada's soil,
    Triumphantly did part,
For love and justice they did toil,
    To reap a peaceful heart.

Peace Offering! Chief Cold Wind invites Blackrobes to set up Missions on Iroquois land

CANTO XVII
Three Blackrobes

Alas dear ones, peace was made,
  The Mohawks learned at last,
Of the French they were afraid,
  Their fighting now had past.

Time had come to pass the pipe,
  To Canada's great surprise,
"Your *Blackrobes* we will now invite,
  Our peacepipe smoke will rise!"

Three *Blackrobes* to their land were sent,
  To plant *God's love* and more,
The seed of faith would make a dent,
  This made their spirits soar.

The Indians cheered and beat their drums,
  When *Blackrobes* did arrive,
A welcome from the Chief had come.
  He smiled but in disguise.

Underneath the Chief's surface,
  Burned hatred all aflame,
Peace was wrapped in his address,
  As flowering words came.

"*Peace and Welcome* to Southern shores,
  This wampum signifies,
Great Spirit ambassadors,
  Your wisdom is our prize!"

"Of Rawennio, your *God* please teach,
     Our Turtle Wolf and Bear,
To our clans freely preach,
     Guide them with your prayer."

"Of life eternal you will learn,
     The true *God* loves us all,
For red and white his heart does burn,
     Gaining *Heaven* is His call."

Tekakwitha listened well,
     To the holy men,
A thought within her soul did dwell,
     "My mother...baptized by them."

The Turtle Chief to them did speak,
     "My longhouse you will stay,"
Tekakwitha, come and meet,
     Fathers Pierron, Frémin and Bruyas."

Chief Cold Wind would treat them well,
     For three days they would stay,
To Tekakwitha he did tell,
     "Prepare a feast today!"

After three days the priests would go,
     To council's Wolf clan,
Hospitality, the Chief must show,
     His daughter's work began.

The Blackrobes in their gowns so black,
     Wearing broad brimmed hats,
Squatting on the bear-skinned mats,
     Midst the buzzing gnats.

The longhouse with heavy smoke was filled,
     With odors of rancid fat,
To sacrifice comforts as God willed,
     The men cheerfully sat.

Kateri Prays   *Elizabeth Wood, 9*

Tekakwitha tried her best,
      To keep her guests happy,
Roast bear meat, the special fest,
      'Twould keep them healthy.

Though feeling sick and nearly faint,
      They ate what was aversion,
This was their offering, to be a saint,
      And bring souls to conversion.

"God bless you child," each did say,
      They finished with a prayer,
Tekakwitha enjoyed their stay,
      Moved by their habits rare.

With heart and soul they said their prayer,
      To captives they were kind,
They brought to souls, *God's love* and care,
      To save them was their find.

While fetching water at the spring,
      She thought of what they said,
Her heart with joy began to sing,
      To know *God* she was led.

The Blackrobe's words she meditated,
      "God is the Father of all men,"
Of his words, she was elated,
      She thirst for *Heaven.*

"Help me to know and love you,
      Great Spirit hear my heart."
Her mother's voice spoke loud and true,
      FAITH BEGAN TO SPARK!

"My mother told me
about those good and
Holy men!"

*Anne as Tekakwitha
McCauley's "Lily of the
Mohawks"*

Song of Kateri...

Princess of the Eucharist

Part II

Tekakwitha Through Teens
To Baptism

Drumbeat

PART II
"Tekakwitha Through Teens"

Tekakwitha through teens saw many cruel scenes,
      Constant battle...sorcerer's rattle,
Shrieking, wailing, fighting, flailing,
      Against torture she turned to see captives burned,
        Tekakwitha's heart churned,
          When she was but a teen.

She lived in turmoil on bloodshed soil,
      Victory celebrations...drinking degradations,
Ritual fire...orgies in mire,
      Of evil she did tire.
        Beauty and grace all afire,
          When she was but a teen.

The *Blackrobe's* words...loving streams,
      Their merciful love...sparkling beams,
They baptized at the stake then *God* the soul would take,
      The Blackrobe was kind, to God he did bind,
        By discipline he lived to *God* he did give,
          When she was but a teen.

Friend or foe, he was ready to go,
      "The God of love they all must know,"
Saviour supreme...on the cross to redeem,
      Nailed by men mean...on a wood beam,
        The true God...her dream...a rainbow was seen,
          When she was but a teen.

An artist of design...the symbol and sign,
      The shell, bead and tapestry,
The Tree of Peace...Hiawatha's dream,
      Eagle atop...her favorite scene.
        A path to measure...the summit her treasure,
          When she was but a teen.

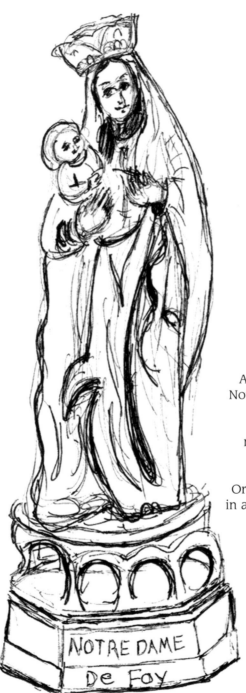

Our Lady of Foy

Notre Dame de Foy

A reproduction of the statue of Notre Dame de Foy was brought from France to the Iroquois Missions in New York in the mid-17th century by the Jesuit Blackrobes.

Originally, it was found encased in a living tree by woodcutters in Belgium.

The Jesuits refer to it as a miraculous statue because many conversions were attributed to it among the Iroqois Indians.

She was invited to see the Nativity,
  Mary and Joseph...the *Holy Family,*
The Babe on straw...afar was the star,
  The crèche serene, and angel scene,
  Tekakwitha amazed...her eyes dazed,
    When she was but a teen.

Notre Dame de Foy, Mother of joy,
  Belgium's statue brought...healings wrought,
A Mission devotion...love in motion,
  Mary with *Newborn*...Tekakwitha was drawn,
  The *Infant supreme*...her eyes did beam,
    When she was but a teen.

A subtle awakening was in the making,
  A spark surging...mystical merging,
A spiritual symphony...a soft epiphany,
  A transcendent state did permeate,
   When a silent voice did sound,
    Calling her to a *virgin's crown,*
     TAKAKWITHA WAS A TEEN!

Mary McCauley, 15

Patrick Wood, 12

Tekakwitha Grinding Corn

CANTO XVIII
Teenage Tekakwitha

Tekakwitha, in teenage years,
    Though shy, she had quick wit,
Her cheery laugh dispelled all fears,
    In play she never FIT.

Her feet did move with inward turn,
    Half blind in light was she,
An artist's soul within did churn,
    A bird in flight was she.

To dance or play was not her style,
    Creating brought her peace,
The woods she trod for many a mile,
    Nature was her lease.

While girls invited braves to dance,
    Tekakwitha by fire squat,
Wampum belts she could enhance,
    Beauty...her genius wrought.

When Tekakwitha was grinding corn,
    She heard some prattle sound,
'Twas her aunts...their voices worn,
    Yelping all around!

"The stubborn girl will not date,
    She'll never dance with boys,
How will she ever find a mate,
    Lacking charm and poise?"

Puppets
"Cook" Yelping!

113

"The Trotter's dance tonight will be,
     Let's dress her for the dance,
She'll have some joyful gaiety,
     A brave she may entrance."

Chief Cold Wind talks to Tekakwitha

Tekakwitha's heart fell low,
     For what she heard them say,
A voice within she did not know,
     Spoke, "Let them have their way!"

Cold Wind met with her to talk,
     To try to do some good
His words to her struck hard as rock,
     She pondered in the wood.

Cold Wind and Cook   *Puppets from McCauley Theatre*

"You can't resist Mohawk tradition,
     To marry, my Princess royal,
Your brave will help my work condition,
     In all the building toil."

"Into our lodge, your brave would come,
     With me he'd give assist,
In game and battle 'til victory won,
     His skills I would enlist."

Spellbound she was left in trance,
     "I'm different than the fold,
My family wants for me romance,
     MY FEELINGS I'LL UPHOLD."

"Her Algonquin origin must be the blame,"
     Cook the aunt did snarl,
Squirrel joined her to complain,
     Tongues from both were foul.

To Cook his wife Cold Wind did snap,
     "STOP YOU IMBECILE!"
Her braids he pulled ...he left no slack,
     Her scream the room did fill!

"Tekakwitha has more sense than you,
     A talented wife she'll make,
Industrious, sweet and docile too,
     A Mohawk brave she'll take!"

"YIELD, SHE MUST," his jaws snapped shut,
     It's time to make a plan,
We'll coax her from this dreadful rut,
     Surely she'll meet her man!

CANTO XIX
Trickery

The family hit upon a scheme,
    A brave for her they'd pick,
A fitting mate to make a team,
    "A-HA...A CLEVER TRICK!"

This was not the way to go,
    The two in love must be,
Parents on both sides must know,
    On marriage they must agree.

The boy and girl will not again meet,
    Until their wedding day,
The ancient custom they must keep
    This was the Mohawk way.

For marriage seal, bride must present,
    A sagamité bowl,
To her groom who will consent,
    To be her loyal soul.

"Okwire"

The Turtle Chief, his pipe did tug,
    As smoke rings curled in air,
His beady eyes looked so smug,
    For the ruse he dare.

A perfect suitor he did choose,
    For his Princess daughter,
She would thank him for this fuse,
    For the brave who sought her.

Princess Tekakwitha   *Peter Jukubcyzk, 7*

CANTO XX
Preparation For The Marriage Rite

The day was set...all signals met,
       The aunts did bustle so,
Suspense in air, no one did fret,
       The plan was sure to flow.

'Twas a day of celebration,
       For the annual Dream Fest,
The Chief possessed a strong fixation,
       To welcome well the honored guest.

'Twas usual for a festive fair,
       For special guests to come,
Tekakwitha was aware,
       So much to be done.

Ceremonial dress was the attire,
       For the princess girl,
Cook with zeal was all on fire,
       To see the wed unfurl.

Purple shells about her neck,
       Strands of wampum beads,
Moccasins, a deerskin set,
       Leggings with sparkling seeds.

White girdle trailing to the ground,
       For a Princess bride,
Though Tekakwitha felt all bound,
       They were satisfied!

All were ready for the call,
　　The guests would soon arrive,
The Turtle Chief stood proud and tall,
　　"SHE'S IN FOR A SURPRISE!"

Footsteps nearing longhouse heard,
　　The dog's barking echoed through,
The bearskin curtain soon was stirred,
　　The guests were in full view.

First the parents welcome given,
　　Followed by their son,
Tekakwitha's smile was hidden,
　　She wished so much to run.

In full regalia, the warrior strode,
　　Tall with mighty gait,
Eagle headdress was his mode,
　　To impress his future mate.

String of elk teeth round his neck
　　On side, fox pelt hung,
When at last the two had met,
　　She thought that all was done.

Okwire beside the Princess sat,
　　She tried to be polite,
Cook had mastered all her craft,
　　'Twas time for marriage rite.

"My Princess dear, do give this bowl,
　　To Okwire for a treat,"
With trembling hands about to dole,
　　Her heart did wildly beat.

A solemn moment...all looked on,
　　The Chief was in suspense,
Tekakwitha felt something wrong,
　　Her body grew more tense.

She dropped the bowl, flew out the door –
all electrified.
McCauley Puppets

In one instance she saw the truth,
      A marriage if complied,
Filled with anger for the ruse,
      Her trembling multipled.

She dropped the bowl, flew out the door,
      All electrified,
Sagamité covered floor,
      Okwire...mystified.

Falling, stumbling in headlong flight,
      While hurting heart bled,
Through field and woods, she ran from sight,
      Behind a tree she fled.

Through her veins hot blood ran,
      Tears did overflow,
"I NEVER WILL MARRY,
      ANOTHER PATH I'LL GO."

Her faithful dog beside her sat,
      For her he pined and whined,
On his head her hand did pat,
      She loved his heart so kind.

Taina Scuderi, 7

Back to the lodge she groped her way,
 Tekakwitha with her dog,
To Great Spirit she did pray,
 "May your sun clear the fog."

They ran through darkness o'er the snow,
 While Dream Fest aired with song,
Tekakwitha would battle through,
 To escape, she knew was wrong.

Rawennio, her mother's God,
 Was her guiding arm,
He will lead with lightning rod,
 Protecting her from harm.

Since Dream Fest was in first phase,
 The lodge would empty be,
She gathered wood for a hearth blaze,
 To keep her family happy.

She missed Enita...gone sometime,
 A convert she became,
Wed to "Onas" a brave so fine,
 "Blackrobes!!"...the Chief did blame.

Tekakwitha was scorned next morn,
 So harsh and cold were they,
She felt that she did not belong,
 But saw a BRIGHTER day!

"Tekakwitha Injures her Foot"   *Lily Maclean, 8*

CANTO XXI
Tekakwitha's Good Luck Injury

She was eighteen years...a sorry lot,
    On the root of a tree, her foot caught,
Tekakwitha's injury...not her fault,
    Gathering wood...providential HALT!

Unable to walk, to her lodge confined,
    Many days of rest, she was resigned,
Weaving, stitching...she spent her time,
    Creating wampums of rare design.

Her uncle went fishing this bright morn,
    Her aunts carried water to field of corn,
Village deserted except sick and the old,
    The *Blackrobe* made calls to his ailing fold.

The curtain was opened, she saw him pass by,
    Tekakwitha's heart burst...her spirit did fly.
"Rakeni," she yelled as she stumbled along,
    The holy priest stunned, he thought he heard wrong!

Father James de Lamberville, in his mind knew,
    The Tortoise Chief's anger at the *Blackrobe's* view,
"Rakeni, come in," her desperate cry,
    Her look courageous...determined her eye.

Fr. James De Lamberville, S.J.

*Francis Xavier in McCauley Theatre
Production "Lily of the Mohawks"*

Tekakwitha described her treacherous fall

The tall priest entered with *Christ* at his side,
    Surprised that the girl's leg was wrapped in hide,
Tekakwitha described her treacherous fall,
    But looked full of joy in her crimson shawl.

The longhouse empty except for a few,
    Just as a thunderbolt out of the blue,
"Teach me Rakeni of your *God* so true,
    I WISH TO BE A CHRISTIAN, I DO, I DO!"

Her face shining in a bright light,
    In his heart he envisioned the girl's sad plight,
Her uncle the Chief would put obstacles great,
    Persecution and suffering would be her fate.

"Nothing will stop me," she cried with zeal,
    "This desire many moons, I did conceal,
My dear Christian mother, a lesson gave me,
    When she traced a cross on a snow-clad tree."

"She told me the tale of the great *Jesus Tree*,
    How Rawennio died for you and for me,"
"'Never forget this lesson I give,
    By the *Cross of Jesus*, we must always live.'"

"Father I want to become a Christian!"
McCauley Family Theatre, Mary as Tekakwitha

"Father, my family can't stop me ...I have my own mind!"
McCauley Family Theatre, from Puppet show "Lily of the Mohawk's

"Each night as I was put to bed,
　　She traced a cross on my forehead,"
"'May the *Great Spirit* love you, my little one,'"
　　"I soon fell asleep...the day done."

"I loved my mother and miss her so,
　　The *God* she loved, I want to know,"
The priest invited Tekakwitha to learn,
　　The truth of faith which she did yearn.

Tekakwitha expressed her will to be taught,
　　"But what if your father forced you to stop?"
She told the *Blackrobe*, she could deal with his rage,
　　"He cannot hinder me, for I am of age!"

"Since against your uncle's will, you dare,
　　When your leg heals, **"baptism...prepare,"**
A new sun shone on this maiden fair,
　　She cried with joy and offered a prayer.

Tekakwitha broke the news that night,
     Her father stared with lips so tight,
Began to smoke...his mind in a rut,
     To his wife and sister, **"keep your mouths shut!"**

The Chief sat silent with face of stone
     The aunts did nothing but moan and groan,
"A CHRISTIAN!" they shrieked, 'tis a reason for slaughter,
     An Algonquin she is...like mother, like daughter!"

While Cook and Squirrel broke out in a din,
     'Twas apparent the news paralyzed him,
As Chief Cold Wind blew smoke rings in the air,
     Tekakwitha asked help to her mother in prayer.

Releasing the child from the grip of his gaze,
     Tekakwitha firm, she let nothing phase,
"A MOHAWK she is, for she'll never bend,"
     The Chief muttered..."HOPELESS, I'M AT MY WIT'S END!"

Tekakwitha broke the news that night!
McCauley from Puppet Show; "Lily of the Mohawks"

Tekakwitha Prepares for Baptism

CANTO XXII
The Great White Feast: Baptism

Her leg healed...lessons began,
    Faith learned in a six month span,
Tekakwitha brilliant with iron will,
    Baptism for *Easter* by Father Lamberville.

The glorious morn burst with song,
    Awakening of a brand new dawn,
The forest birds sang with glee,
    Shrilled *"Hosannas"*...in symphony!

The golden sun shone so bright,
    St. Peter's chapel...colorful sight,
Blossomed trees lined the way,
    Allelulia!...*Easter Day!*

The little bark Church all dressed inside,
    Eager to welcome *God's* new bride,
Garlands and lilies...fragrance sweet,
    The children's choir at highest peak!

Of rough wood walls, beaver skins hung,
    Spears of the hunter and prizes won,
Vivid beads and arrows galore,
    Bright buffalo hides...multi-color!

A bower of green o'er chapel door,
    Bearskin rug covered the floor,
Rafters trimmed with furs of elk,
    Striped blankets and wampum belt!

The altar resplendent with sun's golden stream,
Flowers enhanced by dancing sunbeam,
Non-Christians gathered round the chapel lodge way,
"A **SPECTACULAR** sight!" many did say!

Warriors, hunters, jugglers too,
Brothers, sisters were but a few,
Babes in cradleboards peeked from the back,
Gazing in wonder at the processional track.

"Princess...Reborn!"

The Princess girl, robed in white,
      Donned her baptismal gown,
'Twas Easter Sunday...glowing bright,
      She was light as snowy down.

A blouse and skirt of soft deerskin,
      Transparent veil she wore,
Sash of wampum, blue crosses trim,
      Enraptured, she did soar!

A gentle band, her black braids bound,
      The girl in the white wool shawl,
The cross of *Jesus*, she had found,
      Reborn to never fall!

Around her neck...the "Aves" hung,
      With a cross of gold,
Her soul in ecstasy had sung,
      While hands in prayer fold.

The Princess girl of nineteen years,
      Reborn to never fall,
Pearls rolled down her cheeks in tears,
      The girl in the white wool shawl!

Princess Reborn!
Mary McCauley "Lily of the Mohawk's Puppet Production

CANTO XXIII
Baptism...Procession and Rite

From the forest rim to the chapel door,
      Filled with *God's love* forever more,
Three in procession...downward eyes,
      Through budding trees to be baptized.

Tekakwitha led as they stepped to meet,
      Priest and altar boys to greet,
Birdsong rang from every treetop,
      To the Princess Mohawk...Father did talk.

"What do you ask of the *Church of God?*"
      "Faith," her response in dialogue,
"To what does faith belong?" Next quest,
      "Life eternal," she replied with zest.

"If you wish eternal life,
      Will you obey *God* through strife?"
"Will you love *Him* with all your zeal?
      For your neighbor, this same love feel?"

Filled with God's Love

135

She answered, "Yes," he continued on,
      Ordering all the demons gone,
Tracing the cross on her forehead,
      Prayers to *Holy Spirit* said!

That holy wisdom would fill her mind,
      That *God's pure love* she'd always find,
Grains of salt to taste he gave,
      This symbol of grace, her mind would save.

Her name taken..."Kateri,"
      "Catherine" from Christian history,
Martyr or mystic...either gem rare,
      The reborn soul, in her patron saint's care.

Which Catherine it was, records untold,
      "Alexandria" or "Siena"...either, virtues were gold,
Soon Kateri heard "ENTER...for Christ you will share,"
      A step through the doorway, our Princess was there!"

Baptized Kateri (Catherine)   *Elizabeth Wood, 9*

CANTO XXIV
Kateri Baptized

The "*Great White Feast*" had begun,
    The Mohawk choir, the "*Credo*" sung,
Her head was blessed with sacred oils,
    Satan renounced and all his foils.

Questions were asked on her belief,
    By Father de Lamberville...holy priest,
Saints, sin and Trinity,
    Answered...correctly by Kateri!

Recited she..."*Apostles Creed,*"
    Virtuous life, promised to heed,
On this day of *Resurrection,*
    Immersion in water for perfection.

The choir in glory sang with pride,
    For *Christ* the *Saviour* Who had died,
That Kateri's soul from death would rise,
    Words pronounced, "*I do baptize!*"

Before the birch log font, she knelt,
    Her soul in ecstasy, she felt,
From *Paradise* her mother smiled,
    "*Kateri Tekakwitha my baptized child!*"

Alleluia echoed high,
    From the Chapel to the sky,
Woodland's birdsong all unfurled
    As angel chorus filled the world!

The lily fragrance swept the air,
     This Mohawk flower beyond compare,
Kateri born to never fall,
     This *Easter lily* for children all!

"YOU CHRISTIAN DOG!"

CANTO XXV
Persecution

Because of her new found faith in God,
   She was called by many, "The Christian Dog!"
Sunday was sacred, she refused to work,
   "Tekakwitha!"...her aunts screamed,"A LAZY QUIRK!"

Sundays came...no food to eat,
   Hunger pain...to her was sweet,
She kept a happy cheerful face,
   Remaining firm, 'twas no disgrace.

Children threw cakes of mud,
   At this lovely lily bud,
They mocked and jeered, hurled stones at her
   Her mother's words echoed clear.

"Remember dear, the lesson I give,
   The cross of *Jesus* is what you must live,
He shed His blood on Calvary,
   He died on the cross for you and me!"

The Turtle tribe hissed as she passed,
   "THE CHRISTIAN," while ugly looks cast,
They pushed and shoved...she did not flee,
   She thought of the cross on the *Jesus Tree!*

They mocked and fought...she did not fear,
   The gospel words were loud and clear,
At the foot of the cross did *Mary* stay,
   The *Virgin's* tears would ease her way.

Drunkards tortured with dreadful jeers,
    Enemies of "*The Prayer*" and sorcerers,
Her nerves calm...they turned to steel,
    The *Virgin's presence* she did feel!

Sharp blows on her body, well did tell,
    The scourging at the pillar when *Christ* fell,
Love surged...Kateri's heart afire,
    Sharing in *God's nature* higher!

One day, a brave, eyes ablaze,
    Face distorted...a look of craze,
Lifted his tomahawk...geared to strike,
    She bowed her head...no trace of fright!

Kateri will die for Christ
"She bowed her head...not trace of fright!"

144

Awestruck, amazed...he stared spellbound,
    Her courage unnerved him...fear he found,
Slowly, ferocity died in his eyes,
    He fled with his weapon to her surprise!

Her family and tribe played a big part,
    Trying to dismantle the peace of her heart,
Her willpower was iron, 'twould never bend,
    She offered her suffering that evil would end.

Steadfast she was, through sharp blows and scorn,
    Love was her rose...pain her thorn,
Divine life filled her heart and soul,
    To reach *Heaven*...her foremost goal.

Persecution was her plight,
    Way of the cross to Calvary height,
Her heart burning...for *Christ* she'd die,
    Her flesh tormented...soul high.

An outcast she was to her village around,
    To *God* and her faith...inner joy found,
Thunder, her dog, for her he would fend,
    In forest and river, much time would they spend.

Thunder followed from fields to the spring,
    He wagged his tail while his dear pal would sing,
On a treetop they heard the song of a lark,
    Kateri listened while Thunder did bark.

The loving hound and the Turtle Chief's daughter,
    Often would sit by the Mohawk water,
Kateri would stroke her loyal friend,
    Her faithful dog, she could depend!

Kateri Prays rosary for Safe Journeyt   *Elizabeth Wood, 9*

CANTO XXVI
Flight

No peace of mind had Kateri,
　　　Harassed and tormented by enemy,
Suffering would soon take its toll,
　　　A plan must be made to help this soul.

Father de Lamberville gave this much thought,
　　　A light of wisdom through prayer sought,
"To the Christian village, she must flee,
　　　The Canada mission to be happy."

On the St. Lawrence where waters whirled,
　　　United were *Christians*...faith unfurled,
Converts they were from many a tribe,
　　　Christ's gospel of love, they did abide.

"Francis Xavier" after saint's name,
　　　To Kahnawake many Indians came,
How to get this child to flee,
　　　Caused Father de Lamberville much worry!

God's wondrous ways are gifts sublime,
　　　The priest's prayer answered in His time,
A visit from a great Christian chief,
　　　"Kateri's escape possible"...his belief.

"Glowing Embers"...Chief in the Huron war,
　　　Arrived with Onas, Kateri's brother-in-law,
"Jacob" he brought...his Huron friend,
　　　The two for Kateri, they would fend.

To win souls for *Christ*, from the mission he came,
     "*Garonyage*" meaning "*Heaven*", his real name,
His zeal on fire for pagan conversion,
     This chief brought many to faith immersion.

He once helped with the tortuous killing,
     Of the *Blackrobe Brébeuf*...for *Christ* died willing,
Grace saved the chief from the evil claw,
     Glowing Embers, now Christian, living *God's law.*

Leaving his two friends to complete their plan,
     He spoke at the council of his Oneida clan,
Respected highly as great chief of his nation,
     His oratory on *Christ* aroused emigration.

Onas and *Jacob* planned to meet at midnight,
     Three hoots of the owl...Kateri's cue for the flight,
Her uncle *Cold Wind* was away on trade,
     In Skenedada with the Dutch, much barter he made.

Prayers of thanksgiving as she knelt after Mass,
     The harshness and scorn of her family would pass,
Kateri gazed at the *family* so *holy,*
     She asked protection for her so lowly!

Kateri asks Protection of the Holy Family

Mary and *Joseph* with *Jesus* did flee,
      Bethlehem to Egypt to guard *Baby,*
From Herod who killed each infant boy born,
      Exiled from homeland...their roots torn!

Tears fell as her heart did swell,
      Of memories past...her soul did tell,
Forever she'd leave her valley so green,
      Sadness filled...was it a dream?

The blue-green waters and forest thick,
      Leaving *Thunder* made her sick
Courage given by the *Holy Family,*
      Happiness embraced her suddenly.

To *Father* de Lamberville, Kateri bade,
      A final farewell, then a note he gave,
Sealed to be given to her spiritual guide,
      The contents of which, he did hide.

She returned to her lodge for chores to be done,
      Water from the spring before the noon sun,
Her uncle away, the aunts so mean,
      Though Kateri's face shone...a sunbeam!

With water jug, she left for the spring,
      Thunder followed like a loyal king,
Last time together...Kateri wished to spend,
      Precious moments with her dear friend.

The birds in the forest chirped loud and long,
      Singing to Kateri their lilting song,
The squirrels and chipmunks came out to play,
      To join the party for Kateri's last day!

Kateri and *Thunder* under a cluster of trees,
　　Sat while eating fresh berries,
The Autumn sun looked down to say,
　　"The valley will miss your gentle way!"

After she filled the water jug,
　　She gave her pal a great big hug,
"Don't be sad, when you see me gone,
　　At the *village of prayer,* I belong!"

Thunder barked, he understood,
　　Off they trampled through the wood,
Kateri and her pal...a happy team,
　　The last time for her, in this forest green.

"Don't be sad when I leave you!"　　　*Sara Toman, 6*

Thunder beside as she lay on her mat,
  Tears streamed on his fur as his back she did pat,
Looking down through the roof the midnight moon,
  "Kateri dear, you'll leave very soon!"

Three hoots of an owl, she leaped with a start,
  As silent she could with fluttering heart,
Her moccasins tripped lightly on earthen floor,
  A sign to her dog not to roar.

Thunder's brown eyes showed his sad heart,
  Knowing Kateri was about to part,
"Lie down," she whispered to her dear hound,
  A sign of the Cross...to the forest she bound!

To the rim of the woods, her step did rush,
  Her two protectors appeared from the brush,
Silently the three hurried along,
  Careful their plan wouldn't go wrong!

"Last Time Together:
Anne McCauley as Kateri, "Lily of the Mohawks" Pupper Drama

151

Kateri hid near a big tree

Aidan Wood 4

CANTO XXVII
The Escape

News of escape reached the Turtle Chief's ear,
    From the Dutch post he darted to trap Kateri near,
Through Forest, the trio, well on their way,
    His Princess in secret bound for a new day.

Onas' plan called for play acting,
    To trick the Chief by some distracting,
Her brother-in-law's role...dumb hunter he'd be,
    While Kateri and *Jacob* hid near a big tree.

When the air echoed a bird-call shrill,
    Heard through the trees beyond the hill,
The two would understand the cue,
    That uncle Cold Wind was long out of view.

Turtle Chief's feet ran as swift as a deer,
    Through brush and woods...was Kateri near?
Upon him the moon gazed with a wink
    Behind the hills did its happy face sink.

The chief passed a brave who seemed without wit,
    "He's just a young hunter, no target he'll hit.
Kateri, terrified hidden 'neath leaves,
    Breathless her uncle swept passed the trees.

When path cleared, *Onas* sounded the call,
    No longer was heard Cold Wind's foot fall,
Safety was theirs...the moon had a smile,
    Jacob, Onas and *Kateri* free every mile!

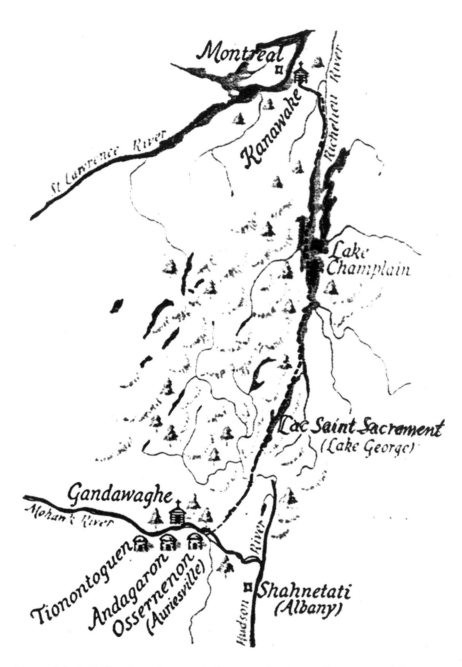

Map of their Difficult Trek *(It took three weeks, 200 miles to cross lakes & rivers to reach the St. Lawrence River)*

CANTO XXVIII
The Difficult Trek

From Mohawk river through forest trail,
      Beyond all danger, they could not fail,
Wings attached to Kateri's feet,
      Her heart in joyful rhythm beat.

Midway in trek, they found their canoe,
      Hidden midst bush and brambles few,
Round rocks and cliffs, the burden they carried,
      With strain of toil, they never tarried.

When night drew its curtain black,
      To eat and sleep, they stopped on track,
Though Kateri's body reeked with pain,
      Not one moment did she complain.

While Kateri nestled under starry sky,
      She prayed in thanksgiving to *God* on high,
As she lay on bed of leaves and moss,
      Though sad for her uncle, she suffered no loss.

Kateri thought of by-gone days,
      To the stars, she lifted her gaze,
Her soul leaped to touch the sky,
      Where diamonds glittered...jewels high.

Her mother's eyes, so clearly seen,
      Enraptured...it was like a dream,
Kateri prayed through starlit trail,
      Then fell asleep to nightingale.

Bound for the "Praying Village"

Deirdre Wood, 7

The new morn brought great hope ahead,
    Bound for the Hudson, the portage they tread,
The sunrise aglow through maple tree,
    With joy they chanted rosary.

As they paddled on Hudson, Kateri's heart soared,
    While rapids, cascades and waters roared,
With the winged creatures, her spirits did fly,
    Herons, falcons and eagles so high.

Fishing and hunting for food they did spend,
    Next bound for lake *Blessèd Sacrament*,
Repose and hunger needs timely met,
    To the Great Spirit their souls would direct.

From Champlain to the North, to the River Richelieu,
    Traveling downstream at risk they knew,
Toward rocks and falls with frightful speed,
    Tossed against boulders, to *God* did they heed.

During the moon of the golden-red hue,
    Finally the sparkling *St. Lawrence* in view,
Two hundred mile trek to Canada's way,
    A new beginning of a sun shining day.

As the *St. Lawrence* widened to lake,
    A thunderous roar o'er rapids did make,
Kateri's eyes flowed with joyful tears,
    Her mother's land dispelled her fears.

The mission with majesty stood on a hill,
    A call to a holier life, *God's will*,
Kateri filled with happiness rare,
    Soon they reached the "*Village of Prayer.*"

Her soul ecstatic at the view,
    Heaven sent...*Jerusalem* new,
From cold raging water, they stopped ashore,
    'Twas peace for Kateri evermore!

"A new beginning of a sun shining day . . ."   Thérese Hundelt, 8

PART III

"Welcome!"

Welcome dear Kateri, to this *Village of Prayer,*
      Here you will find *God's treasures* rare,
Your faith will grow with grace so bright,
      Your song of joy will reach *Heaven's height,*
As the honeybee is nourished from flower to flower,
      God's love will flow as a springtime shower,
Welcome dear Kateri to this kingdom of love,
      You'll find the peace of a turtle dove,
Faith, hope and love will spring from your heart,
      Christ's burning love, you will impart.

Anastasia greets Kateri

Michael Borkowski, 7

Oldest Portrait of Kateri by her Spiritual Director
Fr. Claude Chauchétiere, S.J., 1717

Photo by Anne Scheuerman

The Jesus Tree - St. Isaac Jogues in Exile in his
Woodland Oratory

*St. Thomas Aquinas Church
stained glass window, Nahant, Mass.*

Photo by Marlene McCauley

"Lily of the Mohawks"
Photo by Anne Scheuerman

"Blessed Kateri loved the Holy Eucharist. Just below the stained glass representation of Blessed Kateri is the shining tabernacle. Looking at the window, no one can miss recalling the connection of Kateri's devotion to the Lord in the great Sacrament."

Fr. Joseph McBride, S.J.
Lily, August 1984

Stained glass window of the Longhouse Chapel, facing the Mohawk Valley, Auriesville, N.Y. (a project of Fr. McBride)

Colosseum in background

Photos by Marlene McCauley

Bishop Berthelet blesses Father Alvarez, (Pastor of St. Francis Xavier Mission, Kahnawake). He wears a Kateri stole with the Turtle, Wolf and Bear designed by "Little Peacock" seen on the right. She presented Pope John Paul II same stole at Kateri's Beatification.

Kateri Awards Mass 2004

Marlene's painting (5'x6') "Kateri Children of the World" is seen above doorway.

Front Row: Fr. Jacques Bruyére, Bishop Berthelet, Fr. Alvarez and Deacon Boyer

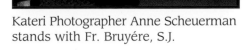

Kateri Photographer Anne Scheuerman stands with Fr. Bruyére, S.J.

Photos by Anne Scheuerman

Bishop Jaques Berthelet of St. Jean, Longueil, Quebec, stands with Vice-Postulator, Fr. Jacques Bruyére, S.J. Missionaries of Charity and the two sets of Kateri Awardees for 2004...Larry & Carol Taylor and Allan & Marlene.

Bishop Berthelet declared 2005, a Jubilee Year for the St. Francis Xavier Mission, celebrating Kateri's 325th Anniversary of her death.

Mohawk Friend
Kateri & Marlene

Kaiatanoron - A Lady of Quality

Kateri's tomb, St. Francis Xavier Mission

Photos by Anne Scheuerman

Albert & Eileen Lazarre, (Mohawks), Kahnawake, Quebec, 2004

Albert has been Kateri's faithful assistant to the Vice-Postulators for over 50 years.

Allan with Canadian Vice-Postulator Fr. Jacques Bruyére, S.J.

Marlene & Allan have wonderful memories of Masses, prayer, singing fests & fiestas honoring Kateri - with Josephine Johnson, Billy Antone and other Tohono O'Odham's, Tucson, Arizona, 1979.

Interestingly on a last visit in the mid '90's, Josephine died a day after Fr. John Paret, S.J. offered Mass at her Mission & blessed she & her family.

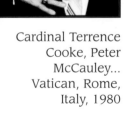

Cardinal Terrence Cooke, Peter McCauley... Vatican, Rome, Italy, 1980

Billy Antone in Rome for Kateri's Beatification, 1980

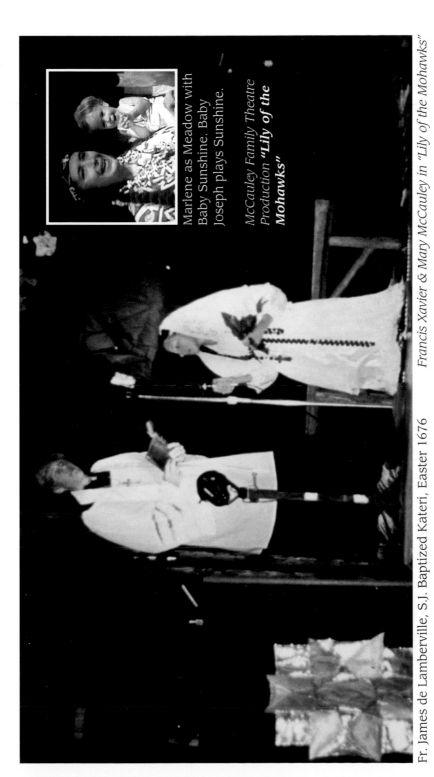

Marlene as Meadow with Baby Sunshine. Baby Joseph plays Sunshine.

McCauley Family Theatre Production **"Lily of the Mohawks"**

Fr. James de Lamberville, S.J. Baptized Kateri, Easter 1676   *Francis Xavier & Mary McCauley in "Lily of the Mohawks"*

Performance in the Colosseum at the Shrine of *"Our Lady of Martyrs"*, July 1976 (after the Eucharistic Congress Show)

Kateri Tekakwitha Adores Jesus in the Blessed Sacrament

Deirdre Wood, 17, Ojai, CA
(see additional art on pgs. 37, 156,
172, 174, 178, and 248)

Pope John Paul II blesses Artist Elizabeth Wood, 2 months. Born May 22, 1985, Rome, Italy. Mary McCauley Wood holds her newborn.

Tekakwitha with her Cornhusk Doll

Elizabeth Wood, 9, Ojai, CA
(see additional art on pgs. 26, 70, 72, 74,
104, 138, 146, 198 and 214)

A New Day

Kateri arrives at the *Praying Village* at the
St. Francis Xavier Mission in Kahnawake, Canada, Oct. 1677

Sean Joseph Wood, 16, Ojai, CA

Monstrance

by Joseph Jukubcyzk, 16,
Ville de Marie Academy, Scottsdale, AZ
(see additional art on page 197)

Kateri, a Mohawk of the Turtle Clan
by Dechelle, 16, an Apache from Cibecue, AZ
A student at Ville de Marie Academy, Scottsdale, AZ

Three Jesuit Blackrobes with two Kateri's (small & big)
Left to right: Thomas More, Francis Xavier, Peter, Mary & Anne

McCauley Family Theatre,
"Lily of the Mohawks" Production

Kateri protects Grandpa Allan (editor), Máire Rose, 8 and Patrick Michael, 12 (artists) from falling into the river!
She also keeps them close to the Cross of Jesus!

Kateri will keep *you* close to the Cross of Jesus also!

See Patrick's art on pages 78 & 112

Máire Rose Wood, 8 in front of mural at San Buenaventura Mission, Ventura, CA

See Máire's art on page 38

CANTO XXIX
Village of Prayer

Anastasia, her "auntie" of many moon's past,
  Smothered Kateri with love..."She's here at last,"
Her stepsister Enita welcomed her too,
  Kateri was home with family true!

Enita's husband Onas, of the trek he did rave,
  "Kateri paddled faster than any brave,"
The Mission encircled by a fort of wood,
  A bastian of faith majestically stood.

To Kateri, Father Frémin did greet,
  "You were eleven when we first did meet,
You dear Princess prepared our meal...
  "Sago, Raguenni...is this all REAL?"

A note she gave from Father de Lamberville,
  The priest read while climbing the hill,
"I send you a treasure, guard it well,
  An angel of *God*, her soul does tell."

Like a bird who found its nest,
  Kateri was finally home,
She labored toward her love filled quest,
  Never again to roam.

Sault St. Louis...Francis Xavier site,
  Were zealous *Blackrobes* three,
To the praying Indians they brought *God's light,*
  Resplendent in Kateri.

Kateri was at home with Enita's Family

Rosalie Simoneau, 9

Father Frémin...Superior
	Cholenec...Spiritual guide,
Humble, mystic Chauchêtière,
	Ever at *Christ's side.*

Kateri loved her family.
	Onas, Enita and boys,
Anastasia...teacher for Kateri,
	Baby's whimper and toys.

She held Enita's baby new,
	Close to her happy face,
To be with faith-filled Christians true,
	A new life to embrace.

A feast prepared of meat and mush,
	Beans and beaver-fat,
Time for prayer...the air was hush,
	Then led to her resting mat,

A wood framed bed with moss on top,
	Blanket of elk hide,
A soft warm skin of stag was brought,
	Wool covers on the side.

Underneath the bed she found,
	A wooden chest of things,
Bundles of ribbons and ringlets round,
	With love that *kindness* brings.

Kateri was moved to happy tears,
	To find her trove of treasure,
Of her support, she had no fears,
	She'd work beyond all measure.

To the *wigwam of prayer,* she wished to go,
	Anastasia led her there,
So different from the cabin low,
	A cross loomed high in air.

A wooden chapel with tower high,
     A sacred edifice,
She entered reverently but shy,
     Knelt in joyful bliss.

Upon the cross her gaze did meet,
     The wounds of *Jesus* five,
Her throbbing heart with love did beat,
     "*You* died that man may rise."

She spent some time in silent prayer,
     With arms crossed at the rail,
She promised *God* while kneeling there,
     To please *Him* without fail.

Soon the two, the Church did leave,
     To make some visitations,
To friends their trod through paths did weave,
     For friendly salutations.

Enroute they met *Father Cholenec,*
     A big smile he did impart,
Kateri's shyness melted away,
     He touched her loving heart.

"Soon you'll learn our praying way,
     Holy Mass and day's devotion,
How we keep sacred *Our Lord's Holy day,*
     You'll set your will in motion."

His words were like a springtime shower,
     Quenching her desert soul,
Explosion of love...a blooming flower,
     Perfection was her goal.

Father *Chauchêtière*, a Jesuit young,
     Gave Kateri a warm welcome,
"*May God bless you...May His will be done,*"
     His words so sweetly rung!

Friends from Ganawagé the two did see,
    The "Great Mohawk" and Satekon
"My wife and I are so happy,
    To this *praying castle* you've come!"

Ganeogowa, this Christian chief,
    Called Kateri, his "niece,"
By grace brought to true belief,
    He and his wife at peace.

These friends so warm filled her heart,
    Their zeal for faith, on fire,
Inspiration to Kateri they did impart,
    That love she did aspire.

Day done, darkness fell,
    Ever grateful for the day,
Her mother's voice in her did tell,
    "I'M WITH YOU ALL THE WAY!

Kateri's family filled
her with love.
Joey Simoneau, 7

"Anastasia: Kateri's Spiritual Mother"

Anastasia, lodge mother, Kateri's mentor was she,
      Of *Saints* and their *sacrifices*, she taught Kateri,
"Store your *virtues* for eternity.
      Replace wampum with your *rosary*,"
Live *Christ's gospel* in charity,
      Prayer and *penance* will set you free,
They are the souls's magic key."
      She guided well the ascetic Kateri,
Who lived her counsel most intensely,
      Imbued with the *Spirit* toward sanctity.

Kateri yearns to receive Jesus in Holy Communion   *Hannah Tesoriero, 8*

CANTO XXX
Yearning For Jesus

Christ the magnet so *Divine*,
    From *Heaven*, living *Bread,*
Kateri's prayer, her gift sublime,
    To *Jesus* she was led.

To live forever was her goal,
    Christ's flesh...eternal life,
From his *Cross, His blood* did flow,
    Eucharist midst strife.

His Sacred Body, bond of love,
    Sacrificed from cross,
Precious gift from *God* above,
    Life's completed course.

Of *First Communion,* the *Blackrobe* said,
    For those baptized anew,
Until on solid ground they tread,
    Must wait for timely cue.

Some deprived for many years,
    While others not so long,
Kateri's love for *Christ* was dear,
    Her faith foundation strong.

To her priest guide she did go,
    Kateri's grace profound,
Her heart on fire...her face aglow,
    The *Holy Table* bound.

Kateri's soul had reached great height,
     At the *Francis Xavier Mission,*
"She is ready, the time is right,"
     Father Cholenec gave permission!

Christmas...sixteen seventy-seven,
     To *God's altar* she would go,
Consuming *Jesus, Bread from heaven*
     Kateri's joy did overflow!

At twenty years baptized by water,
     This Princess child of *God,*
Born the Turtle Chieftain's daughter,
     Soon to receive her *Holy Lord.*

A flame of love for *Christ* will burn,
     Through all eternity,
The fire of love which she did yearn,
     On Christmas morn will be.

A Flame of Love for Christ will burn *Mary Fox, 8*

Kateri makes her First Confession   *Deirdre Wood, 7*

CANTOS XXXI
Kateri's First Confession

Intense was Kateri's preparation,
  For her First *Communion* day,
Promised her *Saviour* reparation,
  For mankind's sinning way.

Mantled in snow, her soul so white,
  Yet unworthy was her thought,
Her purity was her crown so bright,
  To be like *Mary* she sought.

Vanity to her a serious sin,
  When decked in beads galore,
'Twas the custom of her kin,
  She accused herself of more.

Over sin she feared death worse,
  She sadly did regret,
"Sin is death...a wicked curse,"
  Kateri's wisdom set.

Confession perfect she wished to make,
  To the *Holy Spirit* led,
She wished to suffer for *His* sake,
  For her sins her tears were shed.

Kateri's First Holy Communion, Christmas, 1677   *Deirdre Wood, 17*

CANTO XXXII
Kateri's First Holy Communion
Christmas 1677

A new day slowly rose at dawn,
  The last star left the sky,
A little *Babe* in manger born,
  As angels sang on *High*.

As *Christ* was *Prince* in *Mary's womb,*
  A *Tabernacle* live,
Kateri on this Christmas morn,
  Became His Princess bride.

A spotless place within her heart,
  The *Holy Eucharist* blend,
Kateri and *Jesus* n'er will part,
  A fire *He* did send.

His flame will never cease to burn,
  In Kateri's soul so bright,
At last, the *Host* which she did yearn,
  Became her *Sacred Light.*

Lifted she to heights *Divine,*
  To *Jesus* her *True Love,*
Whose *Presence* in her soul did shine,
  With *Trinity* above.

Angels hovered over her,
  As *Brébeuf's hymn was sung,*
*The woodland white...bir*ds astir,
  While Christmas bells rung.

Thou art forever Mine!   *James Milton, 7*

The sun, a dazzling *Host* had spun,
        To welcome the *Infant's birth,*
Born in Kateri, *God's Saviour Son,*
        She was filled with mirth!

Holy Eucharist transformed her soul,
        A burning vessel she,
Rays, resplendent, mystical glow,
        Tears fell joyfully!

Transcendent state of ecstasy,
        'Twas *Christmas* so sublime,
Resounded song of *Kateri,*
        "Thou art forever Mine!"

Kateri sends her Guardian Angel to
Mass to bring her back the Graces

Deirdre Wood, 7

CANTO XXXIII
Great Winter Hunt

Silence hovered o'er the land,
    Christmas season past,
Great hunt venture now at hand
    Kateri's heart downcast.

How could she leave her *village of prayer,*
    Of daily *Mass*...her love,
The poor sick elders were her care,
    What was *His* will above?

Perfume of the pure white snow,
    Fresh air, game and more,
Her family wished for her to go,
    Kateri's vim would soar.

To sacrifice for *Light Divine,*
    'Twas Kateri's solemn vow,
Through dimmed-dark eyes, *God's Light* did shine,
    God's will she would avow.

Through drifts of diamond-speckled snow,
    On snow shoes they did part,
To dense white woods the clan did go,
    Adirondacks...the mark.

The wilderness rang with merry glee,
    As the happy band moved on,
Dancing clouds and mantled tree,
    Soaring eagle through the dawn.

Indian children big and small,
      Braves and women too,
Hunting, feasting, fun for all,
      Three months to renew.

A lesson from the Blackrobe given,
      Before they did embark,
"Work and play by *God* be driven,
      Love *Him* with your heart."

Scrolls of birchbark they did pack,
      Containing daily prayer,
A calendar of feast day fact.
      Faith and grace...their care.

Traveling South were families seven,
      Hauling sleds each mile,
'Till the mountains kissed *God's Heaven,*
      Sun shining with a smile.

By flowing brook at forest rim,
      Would be their camping zone,
A job for each and all the kin,
      Joy was the common tone.

To build the camp, they set to working
      Bark wigwams...the design,
Packing snow while never shirking,
      Smoke through roof did climb.

Half circle dwellings safe from strife,
      Wherein the clans did rest,
A common one for social life,
      Where hunters planned their quest.

Where women cooked and squabbles dealt,
      Families knelt in prayer,
Chatting, singing as spirit felt,
      Children frolicking fair.

Fresh clear air set souls free
        A winter hunt vacation,
Sweet memories for Kateri,
        Wrapped in meditation.

"Oh my *Jesus, God Divine,*
        You are my precious *Dove,*
You filled my soul at *Christmas* time,
        With your *Holy Love.*"

"For one second never leave me,
        An orphan I'd become,
Our love should grow through eternity,
        And *dazzle* as the sun."

Tears in torrents o'er her face did fall,
        For her *Prince Divine,*
To be *His* Princess ever her call,
        United love...sublime!

On the day of *Resurrection,*
        She'd receive a second time,
The winter camp was reparation,
        Her offering would shine.

Her work would be a solemn prayer,
        In union...*Love Divine,*
Kateri brought *God* everywhere,
        His Will in her resign.

When at camp on Sunday morn,
        Holy Mass she missed the most,
A new idea within her born,
        She beckoned her angel host.

Her *angel guardian* she did send,
        To the "*Praying Village*" Mass,
While she to all her chores tend,
        Return he with graces fast.

Kateri's secret woodland oratory
"She knelt in drifting snow..."

While all the family snugly slept,
  Rosary she prayed,
With consuming love she wept,
  'Till fire to embers made.

For hours few she fell asleep,
  Dreaming of her *song...*
Her *Eucharistic Host* so meek,
  The Princess girl did long.

Before the morn was born anew,
  Kateri slipped outside,
Into artic air so blue,
  To *Jesus* crucified.

She carved a cross on a white-robed tree,
     Knelt in drifting snow,
Hidden in secret oratory,
     Kateri's soul aglow.

The Jesus Tree, the Jesus Tree,
     He died for you and me,
The Jesus Tree, the Jesus Tree,
     Her childhood memory.

The cross alit with snow and ice,
     Shone brilliantly with rays,
Redeeming King, He bore the price,
     For man's eternal days.

As sun doth rose, the cross hung red,
     Glistening with the frost,
The piercing wounds of *Jesus* bled,
     One soul should n'er be lost.

She hastened through the snowbound scene,
     Back to winter camp,
While all the sleepers lay in dream,
     She to *God* did thank!

The breakfast meal she did prepare,
     Her workday now began,
A hot sagamité fare,
     For the hungry clan.

The Brave Hunters

CANTO XXXIV
The Hunter's Day

The forest woke in merry song,
    A medley filled the air,
Barking dogs and laughing throng,
    Ready for the fare.

Meal prepared with love and care,
    Fish, fat and meat,
Eaten after morning prayer,
    With sagamité treat.

An enormous meal for the men,
    Devoured until content,
A hunt to burrows, lairs and den,
    High energy was spent.

When braves departed for the hunt,
    Hard labor did begin,
Women ready for the stunt,
    The animals to skin.

Raccoon, elk or caribou,
    Stag, moose or bear,
Waiting patiently for the cue,
    The brave with tricks did dare.

In that time of desperation,
    He'd blow a birch-bark horn,
To sound a cry of imitation,
    Luring prey to song.

'Twas his mate...a welcomed croon,
	Thinks of love's romance,
Following the path of doom,
	Dead by arrow's lance.

The hunter's tracks were etched in snow,
	A guide where game was found,
Where Kateri and her friends would go,
	To drag the beast around.

Through icy drifts the way was slow,
	With elk in its demise,
Tired and weary they filled their role,
	Helping with the prize.

The women scraped the pelts and furs,
	Rubbed the tanning paste,
'Twas great fun," they did concur,
	Nothing went to waste.

The Hunter's Prize

The women scraped the pelts and furs . . .

Deer-brains and moss mixed as one,
      The paste put onto hide,
Over fire to dry they hung,
      Spoils were to divide.

Older girls joined the team,
      They butchered with great skill,
Meat from deer so rich and lean,
      With others from the kill.

Many tummies to daily serve,
      Some meat they had to store,
Days when hunter's luck would swerve,
      No game in sight to lure.

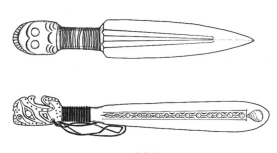

The hunter was daily put to test,
     Bravely they did comply,
Except for Sunday...day of rest,
     Meat eaten from supply.

The winter chase...the hunter's deed,
     A fierce courageous quest,
This noble cause fulfilled the need,
     To give the clan a fest.

Giggling, wriggling, rollicking round,
     Dancing, mingling, singing sound,
Children playing, jumping bound,
     Chatting, gossiping women found!

When unkind words were sometimes said,
     Of *God*, Kateri her thoughts were led,
To *Saints* and *prayer* and holy mind,
     She raised them to heights *Divine*.

When sky aglow with sunset's flame,
     Then *feasting* after prayer,
Thanking Rawennio for the game,
     And *His* wondrous care.

A calm descended o'er the camp,
     For all...a day's work done,
Great Spirit lit the dark sky's lamp,
     United...all were one!

Squatting by the fire they sat,
     The hunter's pipes in hand,
Planning well next day's attack,
     The bravely battling band!

"A Vicious Rumor"

A lance had pierced her bleeding heart,
      Of Kateri's pain this verse will tell,
Gossip etched a cutting mark,
      A vicious rumor on her befell,
Her innocence challenged by defamation,
      Christ's cross-suffering...consolation,
He, the *God-man*...humiliated,
      King and *Saviour*...annihilated,
From *His wounds, His blood* flowed,
      While love gushed forth and mercy glowed,
Bright red rays...*His love-compassion,*
      Dazzling white...*purification,*
For *Christ* she bore her *flagellation.*

Christ's cross-suffering Kateri's consolation
Cross in Auriesville, N.Y.; Martyr's Shrine

"Slander"

A Brave...good *Christian*...integrity great,
  Hunting a moose, he arrived home late,
His bones so weary...exhausted his state,
  Blinking and blurring...first mat he did take,
The space was not his...it wasn't his mate,
  'Twas Kateri asleep...he made a mistake,
His wife convinced he was a flake.
  Fury betook her with anger and hate,
Among her friends, she did Kateri berate,
  The mistrusting shrew caught another view,
When her husband asked help to build a canoe,
  In this art, skillful people were few,
He called upon Kateri for stitching to do,
  His wife concluded that he was UNTRUE,
Though a woman she was of fine reputation,
  Against Kateri's innocence her accusation,
'Twas a vicious allegation,
  Causing Kateri devastation.
Heart-stricken was Kateri...she had no peace,
  "Would this gossip ever cease?"
She never believed that a woman of prayer,
  Would be capable of slander...how could she dare?
Vowed Kateri, this her LAST HUNT she affirmed,
  For the spiritual life her soul burned,
Mass, Benediction and *prayer* she yearned,
  Her accuser she prayed for,
Holy forgiveness she learned.

A Mistrusting Gossiper

190

"Kateri Vindicated"

The vicious rumor reached its peak,
      When Father Frémin, the *source* did seek,
To him the issue she told with heat,
      He met with Kateri holy and meek,
The truth was told, she'd not retreat,
      Impurity denied...defense complete.
"I would never sin against my *love*,
      I vow to my *God* in *Heaven* above
The priest's conclusion was concrete,
      "Kateri's soul is grace replete,
Her virtue pure as lily sweet."
      Several years later when the saintly girl died,
For slander...the accuser for many moons cried,
      She begged *God's justice* satisfied,
Through Kateri's mercy...soul sanctified.

"I would never offend
God in any way!"

Eric Simoneau, 6

191

Second Holy Communion, Easter, 1679   *Elizabeth Wood, 9*

CANTO XXXV
Happy Homecoming
Easter, 1679: Kateri's Second Communion

A happy homecoming for Kateri dear,
     In the depths of her soul still the thrust of the spear,
Away from the Mission, for her an exile,
     Holy Mass and the *Cross* changed her tears to a smile.

Returning from hunt, *Holy Week* drew near,
     Of her recent thorn, Kateri shed her last tear,
Grateful she was for exoneration,
     The pain was food for reparation.

Anastasia repeated her exhortation
     For *Christ's passion,* do mortification,
Implore *God's mercy* for our nation's conversion,
     For their sins of dread perversion.

Kateri's resolve...*Christ's pain* to immolate,
     'Till her last breath 'twas her apostolate,
For her people's souls to regenerate,
     In time...to *God* they would venerate.

A wild courage in Kateri...manifesting,
     Insatiable thirst for extreme suffering,
A spiritual battle unceasing she fought,
     For the salvation of souls she sought.

With *Jesus* on *His Cross* she did belong,
     To suffer with *Him* was her soul's song,
To taste the gall of *Calvary,*
     And lead sinners to immortality.

To *Jesus* in *Eucharist*, her soul she would give,
    Her body, a crucible that she may live,
Her suffering a means for purification,
    She'd be one with her *Lover's crucifixion*.

A triduum of silence, then bells did toll,
    A glorious sound for Kateri's soul,
Her second *Communion* she would receive,
    After three months of longing she couldn't believe.

'Twas *Easter* morn sunny and bright,
    The woodland sang...a sheer delight,
The angel choir broke out in song,
    "Alleluia...*Christ* rose this morn!"

Colorful flowers did abound,
    Fragrance of lilies all around,
Evergreen branches...altar decorated,
    Resurrection...recreated!

Flickering candles all aglow,
    Clouds of incense drifted slow,
Children's choir sang with glee,
    Christians thronged happily.

White surplices and robes of red,
    Six altar boys with candles...tread,
To assist the priests at *Easter Mass,*
    A privilege no lad could surpass.

Father Chauchêtiére...the Gospel read,
    How *Lord Jesus* rose from dead,
Father Cholenec...his sermon taught,
    "Death is life...*God's mercy* wrought."

To the *Sacred Banquet,* Kateri did go,
    Her tears of love did overflow,
She deemed herself lowly and least,
    Exalted, at *His Holy Feast.*

Her soul a ciborium for the *Most High*,
   Light as a feather, she felt she could fly,
On Sundays and Holy Days, she'd receive her *Guest*,
   With her heart's *Lover* she was her best.

Hosannas rang with joyous strain,
   Christ forever *He* would reign,
Mass concluded...all aflame,
   A great surprise...the next day came!

Father Frémin sought Kateri,
   Convinced she...an *"angel of charity,"*
Invited her to be of the *Holy Family,*
   Kateri ecstatic felt unworthy.

To be one of this pious congregation,
   A tribute to virtue of resignation,
She flushed with joyful exhilaration,
   A path toward her sanctification.

A member made she by *Blackrobes* three,
   The sick, the dying and enemy...
She'd serve and pray for happily...
   The *Holy Family* rosary.

Kateri is invited to join the
Holy Family Assn.

195

Bishop Laval, this confraternity,
　　　He set for spirituality,
Jesus, Mary and Joseph...for family,
　　　Consecrated to them, the members be.

All over Canada, it spread like fire,
　　　Sister Brésoles, she did inspire,
A *saint* and this *holy association*,
　　　"*One and the same*"...the exhortation.

Each Sunday the group met for meditation,
　　　For Kateri...a dedication,
This precious gift...to her given,
　　　To continue toward Heaven...she, driven.

Kateri's Second Communion

After Kateri received her Second Holy Communion, she was allowed to receive Jesus on Sundays and Holy days. This law of the Church was revised when Pope Pius X, during his reign 1904-1914, urged the laity to receive frequent Holy Communion.

"Kateri's Path to Heaven"

In virtue Kateri achieved mastery,
      The jewel of her crown was purity,
She bonded with *Blessèd Virgin* intimately,
      Kateri thought herself unworthily,
She scourged herself unmercifully,
      She branded her foot painfully,
Stepped barefoot on snow so icily,
      She slept on thorns in agony,
Prayed in the cold chapel unceasingly,
      Attended two Masses early,
She chanted the rosary faithfully,
      She tended the sick so cheerfully,
She gave all to the poor so graciously.
      Her chores were done exquisitely,
She spoke to all angelically,
      Her smile shone radiantly,
She gazed at the cross so tearfully,
      Prayed for her nation devotedly,
In her secret woodland oratory,
      She knelt at her *Jesus Tree,*
In her secret woodland oratory,
      She prayed so mystically,
In her secret woodland oratory,
      She contemplated *Calvary*.

Joseph Jukubcyzk, 16

Kateri and Teresa are best of friends,
they pray and do penance together.

Elizabeth Wood, 9

CANTO XXXVI
Kateri Meets a Friend

On the steep riverbank in the brisk fresh air,
    The wood cross stood so high,
Tekakwitha knelt to *God* in prayer,
    When a friendly girl came by.

"Excuse me Kateri Tekakwitha,
    I wish to be your friend,
My name is Mary Theresa Tegaiaguenta,
    To you my *God* did send."

Soon did the two, their spirits blend,
    Each her story told,
Prayerful moments they would spend,
    Their friendship did unfold.

"I know you are a holy girl,
    Your help I sorely need,
I wish my soul to be a pearl,
    God's heart I've caused to bleed."

"Like a turtle I am slow,"
    Responded Kateri,
"I'll try to be your Christian role,
    Praying is the key."

Theresa felt more secure,
    To tell her life's history,
Kateri's patience did endure,
    To see her friend's soul free.

"Though baptized at fifteen years,
     My faith I did not live,
A pagan spouse filled me with fears,
     To Satan I did give."

"Pleasure loving took first place,
     Drinking made me dizzy,
The "Black Dance" cult I did embrace,
     Sinning kept me busy."

"This *Praying Village* did my sister come,
     God's grace began to flow,
With her came her little son,
     A NEW LIFE WE HAD TO KNOW!"

"My husband and I left with them,
     To change, I resolved,
Soon I made a good confession,
     My sin was all dissolved."

"My good intentions fell apart,
     Drinking I resumed,
Satan again sealed his mark,
     Forever I felt doomed."

"Another chance *God* gave to me,
     'Twas on a winter hunt,
My husband's death made me see,
     My life a ribald flunk."

"My sister's son and I were spared,
     The fight against starvation,
'Twas a miracle how we fared,
     I promised reparation."

"Yet firewater still is my vice,
     No matter how I try,
I hate my sin...yet it taste so nice,"
     Theresa breathed a sigh.

Kateri's arm round friend embraced,
    "You told your story well,
Your drinking habit will be erased,
    A strong WILL POWER shall!"

Kateri and Theresa soul-mates became,
    Helping each to *Heaven*,
Though each unlike, they thought the same,
    Jesus was their leaven.

Acts of penance the two performed,
    In fields they worked and prayed,
Theresa's life became reformed,
    Her drinking past did fade.

"June...Moon of Strawberries"

Bursting with life...the *Strawberry Moon,*
    When days were sunny and long,
Seed blessed the last time in June,
    On the Chapel altar that morn.

The new Church would open the next harvest feast
    First fruits on new altar would be,
Joy filled the hearts of the *Blackrobe* priests,
    Harvesting souls...God's *royal plea!*

Fire-fishing held Kateri's fascination

CANTO XXXVII
Deer of the Water and Fire Fishing

The **"deer of the water"** swam swiftly upstream,
    Against the rapids sped,
Into the nets of the fishermen seen,
    Trapped...for mouths to be fed.

Giggled Theresa to her pal Kateri,
    "You are like the water deer,
You swim upstream toward eternity,
    God's love forever near."

"You never get caught in the net of sin,
    Virtue is your goal,
Many souls for *God* you'll win,
    You are model role."

Fire-fishing held Kateri's fascination,
    A torch in the black of night,
Held in the stern for illumination,
    Fish attracted by light.

To the surface the fish come,
    Speared...tossed in canoe,
Nailed to cross...*Christ's mission* done,
    He died for me and you.

To light a candle in the dark,
    God's rule we must conform,
Our love for *Christ* sets a spark,
    Enkindling fire...RE-BORN!

Kateri is like the "water deer", she
swims upstream toward eterinty!

Visit to Ville Marie

CANTO XXXVIII
Visit to Ville Marie

Into canoes ready to leave,
      An array of wares to take,
Belts and baskets some did weave,
      Crafts they did create.

'Twas summer sixteen-seventy eight,
      Excitement at its peak,
For Theresa and Kateri...a special date,
      Adventure they would seek.

Paddled canoes for Ville Marie,
      Named..."*Mary's Village*" well,
A new journey for Kateri,
      To barter goods and sell.

From a distance they could see,
      The cross on the mission site,
The forest dwindled to a tree,
      The rapids swirled with might.

When they arrived...saw buildings tall,
      To Kateri's wonderment,
An area of surrounding wall,
      From Iroquois raids...defend.

She began to dream when battle fought,
      Ossernenon all ablaze,
For the French...a victory wrought,
      For Mohawks fighting craze.

Planted well the *Blackrobe Cross,*
  Peace was then proclaimed,
Mohawks suffered not one loss,
  Not a warrior maimed.

Peace pipe passed...treaty drawn,
  Blackrobes welcomed in,
For *Christian* faith...a brand new dawn,
  For many souls to win!

Kateri's face shone with glee,
  That she was led thus far,
She loved her mother's faith-country,
  It was *God's guiding* star.

A tap on the back by her fun-filled friend,
  Brought Kateri back to earth,
"When and if we've time to spend,
  We'll explore this turf!"

St. Paul's street teemed with life,
  With Indians of the *"Prayer,"*
The townsfolk came...man with wife,
  Crowds from everywhere!

The two friends set up their display,
  At the market place,
To sell their goods for needs to pay,
  From the craft-filled case.

Deerskin items packed in bin,
  Embroidery of rare design,
Glass wampum belts and moccasin,
  Created by hand so fine.

When goods were sold...they took a break,
  To make good use of time,
An interesting tour they'd take,
  To see some sights sublime.

Kateri's eyes scanned all directions,
　　　To see a style so strange,
Symbols of a civilization,
　　　An eye-opening change.

Dwellings built of wood and stone,
　　　In front...a sturdy door,
Different from the longhouse dome,
　　　With its earthen floor.

From St. Joseph's street to the square,
　　　Their happy feet did trod,
Their eager eyes became aware,
　　　Of a house of *God*.

Root foundation for *Notre Dame,*
　　　Cathedral of grandeur,
Today it is of world-wide fame,
　　　Near was Hôtel-Dieu.

They stopped to rest for a pleasant while,
　　　On lush green grass they sat,
Observing colonists pass with style,
　　　With shirt and straw-brimmed hat.

They viewed the mount that loomed ahead,
　　　"Mont-Royal"...Montreal,
Theresa to her pal had said,
　　　"LET'S VISIT THE HOSPITAL!"

Ville Marie when Kateri dreams of
the battle when the French
attacked the Mohawks, 1666

Kateri saw Nuns for the first time!

CANTO XXXIX
Visit to Hôtel Dieu

The Hôtel Dieu was close on *"Rue,"*
    Kateri filled with awe,
To meet a group she never knew,
    Who followed a special law.

Kateri and Theresa knocked at the gate,
    Suspense was in the air,
The door opened...not a wait,
    A girl in white, there.

Their cross she saw...invited them in,
    You're from the *"village of prayer,"*
A smile that lit her face did win,
    Kateri so fair.

She asked if they wished to tour,
    The hospital this time,
She'd take them through Hôtel Dieu,
    Kateri's face did shine!

"Assontaté," if you permit,
    Théresa replied happily,
Kateri's eyes so sparkling lit,
    To feel her charity.

Beyond the enclosure of palisades,
    Through the buildings of wood,
Bustling were the paleface maids,
    Serving as they could.

Many questions were in store,
        Of this friendly nun,
Kateri's soul began to soar,
        To see *God's will* be done.

The women lived as one family,
        Husbands never had,
Their lives enchanted Kateri,
        Alike in white were clad.

They nursed the sick and fed them well,
        Gave them medicine,
Stopped to pray at sound of bell,
        Helped bandage injured limb.

Explanations cleared her mind,
        About the single state,
Only *God*, Kateri wished to bind,
        He'd be her *eternal mate*.

"To give one's life, a gift of love,
        To *Jesus* for *His* sake,
Priests and nuns, called from above,
        God's kingdom they do make."

Kateri sang in jubilation,
        At the explanation,
A nun she'd be...Kateri,
        The two left happily.

Kateri prays at Heron Isle for direction

Elizabeth wood, 9

"Plan of Life"

From Ville-Marie, Theresa and Kateri,
　　　Emotions high...could touch the sky,
'Twas a startling revelation
　　　For Kateri's life...clarification,
To learn of women in single state,
　　　Explained why she never wished a mate,
Vows of poverty and chastity,
　　　Nourished nuns growth in sanctity,
Obedient to Superiors all,
　　　Religious vocation..."*God's call,*"
"Nuns" to God...dedicated
　　　By prayer and grace...illuminated,
Lived together in community,
　　　Helping poor in charity,
Tending sick so lovingly,
　　　Frequent confession...souls clean,
Part of convent's holy routine,
　　　Dressed alike in habits white,
Always wore a smile so bright,
　　　Gardening, baking, hospital care,
Perfection sought for virtue rare,
　　　A humble dwelling they lived in,
So *God* they could give *Him*,
　　　By prayer, dispelled sin,
For many souls to win!
　　　These nuns...models to imitate,
For Kateri and Theresa to emulate,
　　　Their lives to *God* they'd consecrate
To follow holy rules...couldn't wait,
　　　A "*Plan of life*" to enact in haste,
There were not minutes to waste!

Kateri wants to become a Nun and start a Convent

Anna Van Hecke, 13; Santa Paula, CA

CANTO XXXX
"A Convent on Heron Isle"

Kateri and Theresa by the Cross met,
    To talk of thoughts sublime,
"Nuns" dream...minds set,
    To give to *God Divine.*

To invite a third girl, they agreed,
    For a community,
Evangelical counsels they'd heed,
    Bound by sanctity.

Kateri asked...who might this be?
    Right girl Theresa knew,
"A holy woman,"..."Marie,"
    To vows she would be true."

"She lived a convent life one time,
    Spending hours in prayer,
Her discipline and goodness fine,
    Make for virtues rare."

To join the team, Marie agreed,
    Together, *God* they'd serve,
Convent rules, they would heed,
    Of vows they would not swerve.

They'd dress alike...pray as one,
    Convent home must find,
Brides of Christ they would become,
    In truth, they'd not be blind.

217

The trio found the "ideal" place,
     'Twas on Heron Isle,
A haven for them to *God embrace,*
     Each face lit with smile.

Kateri pondered for awhile,
     Then her advice she gave,
"Let's not be led by Satan's guile,
     And fall into his maze."

To do *God's will*...solemn prayer,
     Obedience...their vow,
Subject to Father Frémin's care,
     Could they seek his approval now?

To the *Mission*, Teresa was sent,
     Their story she did tell,
Of ideas for a new convent,
     He listened with attent.

The plan to him she did outline,
     Then asked for his consent,
Led by prudence, he could not assign,
     Though praised their good intent.

"My wisdom dear, please take heed,
     Though you have no fear,
'Tis dangerous where your dreams do lead,
     For good, I interfere!"

"You may have your high ideal,
     But experience you lack,
Practice here your faith and zeal,"
     The Blackrobe spoke with tact.

Through the priest, *God's will*...the sign,
     To give up the convent life,
Very clear was *His* design,
     Protection from all strife.

When Father's reasons enumerated
     The three girls...resonated...
"To live lives...sanctificated,
     All for *God*...venerated,

Faith-filled life...radiated,"
     Rendered them...consolated,
"To never marry"...Kateri annunciated,
     "To offer *widowhood,*" Theresa stated.

Kateri's family nag her to marry

Hannah Tesoriero, 8

"Another Thorn!"

About to turn twenty-three,
      Was holy, gentle Kateri,
Determined to live in celibacy,
      Harrassed by unreasonable family,
Enita bold to Kateri told,
      "Still time to have a happy fold,
My sister PLEASE MARRY,
      No more should you tarry,
A warrior-brave you should wed,
      You'd be ahead,
          All would be fed,
          Your family well led
"Respect" for you, said,
      "A warrior-brave you should wed!"
Kateri's ear bent with chagrin,
      By darts from her kin,
          Cut like a blade,
          Kateri dismayed,
The vitriol never did fade!
      "Kateri, TIS YOUR OBLIGATION,
To help by compensation
      Our longhouse sustenation."
Spoke Kateri with calm patience,
      "My creations enable my sharing,
          God helps me when I'm praying,
          Trusting like the birds of air,
Rawennio watches with care,
      "God won't abandon me in flight,
I love *Him* with all my might!"
      "Pray Kateri," Enita said,
"May *God* put SENSE into your head!"

Kateri decides to never marry
She wants her spouse to be Jesus

Tess Mullins, 14

CANTO XXXXI
Kateri's Resolution

To Father Cholenec, Tekakwitha did go,
      To speak of what transpired,
Of how Enita's diatribe did flow,
      Until worn out and tired.

"'Tis clear she lacks understanding,
      Of my single state,
She spends much time complaining,
      That I should take a mate!"

"*Jesus* is my only love,
      To *Him* I give my life,
He will help me from above,
      And protect me from all strife.

Astonished was the *Blackrobe* priest,
      At convert Kateri,
Of *God's flock*, the humble and least
      Desires celibacy.

The priest put Kateri through the test,
      To see if she was sincere,
Convinced she was a pure heart blessed,
      For her he had no fear.

"*God* will provide and help me earn,
      His grace will multiply,
To give my life to *Him* I yearn,
      For *Him* I'll live and die."

"Go with *God* dear Kateri,
     Spend some time in prayer,
If you choose virginity,
     He'll keep you in *His* care."

Consoled she was with attitude,
     She felt nearer to her goal,
She knelt in *Church* with gratitude
     Begging *God* to guide her soul.

By prayer and penance she'd prepare,
     A single life to live,
In holy purity...a state so rare,
     Unstained soul to *God* she'd give.

This she prayed her family accept,
     That *His holy will* be kept,
Her duty to them would be met,
     Empowered by *love*, she wept.

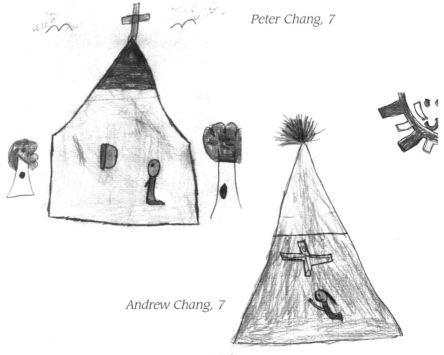

Peter Chang, 7

Andrew Chang, 7

"More Agitation"

A few weeks later when Kateri seated,
    Issue of marriage again repeated,
Anastasia joined Enita with harassing,
    Exploding, scolding, warnings, blasting,
Righteous indignation,
    Dreadful accusation,
Poor Kateri...dreadful scene,
    "STUBBORN"...the matriarch did scream,
Full of stress and painful strain,
    Kateri's heart was in distain.
Out of the wigwam Anastasia did storm,
    To tell the priest of Kateri's wrong,
To Tekakwitha...another thorn,
    For soul's freedom, she did long,
Only to **God** did she belong.

The family scolds Kateri
for not marrying
Anthony, 7

Kateri is a Free Spirit
Her family accepts her decision to be married to Jesus.

CANTO XXXXII
"Free to Fly"

When Anastasia left, Kateri wept,
      Her tears would water stalks of corn,
A voice within spoke, "Don't forget,
      A new hope rises in the morn!"

The wind was swirling, whirling round
      Anastasia to the priest was bound.
A litany of invectives...erupted,
      Father Cholenec...uninterrupted.

Of impatience, he gave no sign,
      Stroked his beard with calm,
When she finished he spoke a line,
      "Kateri has done no harm!"

"To embrace chastity all her days
      Will merit sanctification,
Kateri deserves the highest praise,
      For seeking single vocation."

"You a Christian should not condemn,
      Her holy state of love,
This will be your path to *Heaven*,
      Encouraging YOUR pure white Dove."

"To your charge, you must act kind,
      Her single life...appreciate,
Kateri Tekakwitha has a strong mind,
      God is her **only** mate!"

Anastasia stood numb...a heavy blow,
       She saw her error...her mind clear,
"Kateri's graces do overflow,
       Anointed daughter dear!"

She sobbed and sobbed at her mistake,
       Causing Kateri pain,
She and Enita...reparation would make,
       Themselves they had to blame.

When Kateri from the field returned,
       She saw a transformation,
A peaceful love burned within her,
       For Kateri...restoration!

All powers of her soul were free,
       Perfection she would strive,
By prayer, suffering and charity,
       Her soul to *God* would rise.

Now that all the turmoil ceased,
       Her *SOUL* she'd give...*God's Sacred Feasts,*
To her *Jesus* **crucified**,
       She'd give her *BODY*, agonized

In her secret woodland oratory
Kateri prayed at her Jesus Tree.

Katya Nicols & Sage Cody, 13

Kateri decides to take a vow of Virginity on March 25 - Feast of the
Annunciation

CANTO XXXXIII
"Vow: The Date"

January...sixteen-seventy-nine,
    Winter hunt at hand,
Kateri would not go this time,
    Chose she..."*mission*" land.

All had urged Kateri go,
    Well fed her body be,
Fresh air 'twould give her healthy glow,
    She wished her soul free.

"When the body nourished well,
    The soul will languish so,
When hunger sets...the soul can tell,
    That *Jesus' love* doth flow."

Though FARE profuse and brisk air fine,
    Tekakwitha's joy was "home,"
Penance, works and *prayer Divine,*
    To field and church did roam.

With *Jesus Christ,* she well fed,
    Within her soul *His Life,*
Holy Communion was her *Bread,*
    Through joy, pain and strife.

The *Blessèd Sacrament* she adored,
    Five times a day,
Though frail in body, her spirit soared,
    From *God*, she'd never stray.

A meeting planned, the priest would see,
　　　　Kateri...to inquire,
Of this *"angel of charity,"*
　　　　"What was her soul's desire?"

Aware that she was filled with fire,
　　　　Father Cholenec did ask,
"Your virgin soul for *Christ* aspire?"
　　　　"Yes," she answered fast.

"More than ever," she replied,
　　　　"Please let me take a vow,
As nuns do at Ville-Marie," she sighed,
　　　　He:..."To enter convent...HOW?"

He knew she'd have to read and write,
　　　　With Kateri...no fear,
She:...imbued with *Spirit's Light,*
　　　　"Could I take my vow HERE?"

"Do I need an education,
　　　　To live with family?
Would *Jesus* bind my declaration,
　　　　Of perpetual virginity?"

"With your family, you may live,
　　　　A life of celibacy,
To *Jesus Christ,* your soul will give,
　　　　You'll grow in sanctity."

Seeing Kateri's determination,
　　　　Gave his approbation,
For her life of abnegation,
　　　　Vow set...*Annunciation!*

"Just three months from today,
　　　　A vow you'll have made,
With *Our Lady* you will say,
　　　　'*I am the Lord's handmaid!*'"

"Joy" her soul...permeated,
     Divine Love burst within,
March twenty-fifth anticipated,
     The Princess' Spouse to win.

The Blackrobe felt consolation,
     The vow will be fulfilled,
"Until that time, make preparation,
     For the gift *God-willed.*"

"Thank you *Father*," she did cry,
     In me God will *increase,*
I am nothing," she did sigh.
     I simply will *decrease.*"

Kateri gave her body to Jesus on the Cross and her soul
to Jesus in the Holy Eucharist

"Angel of Charity"　　　　　　　　*Kateri Lemmon, 15; Santa Paula, CA*

CANTO XXXXIV
Angel of Charity

Through village paths, Kateri did go,
    To visit needy band,
To wigwams twelve, her love aglow,
    To give her helping hand.

She stopped to visit sick and old,
    Brought them food and wood,
While combing, oiling hair, she told,
    Faith stories as she could.

To the lonely she brought joy,
    Their pain she helped to ease,
With the moody, she did employ,
    A loving way to please.

Their cot she set...tucked them in,
    Kissed, then said a prayer,
"Dear Lord, bless this dear woman.
    Send her angel fair."

When all her visitations done,
    Off to chapel trod,
She burned with love to *Jesus-Son,*
    And for her *Father-God*.

A penitential belt she wore,
    While happiness gained,
For *Christ's passion* she did endure,
    Agonizing pain.

Her work she softened with her prayer,
     She built her prayer with work,
To speak to *God*...love to share,
     For *Him,* she hid all hurt.

She spent hours in contemplation,
     Of her *Love*, day and night,
In *Eucharistic adoration,*
     Jesus...her delight.

The bite of cold when oft she knelt,
     Subdued by *fire of love,*
Kateri despised herself,
     Filled with *God* above.

The *Queen of Virgins,* she ascribed,
     Her gift of charity,
She with *Mary* identified,
     Angelic *chastity*.

To the lonely, Kateri brought joy. She helped the sick and poor. She was an "angel of charity".

Alyssa Henry, 16

236

Kateri teaches children to Love God

Anna Van Hecke, 13
Santa Paula, Ca

Jesus Christ became Kateri's Princely spouse on the Blessed Virgin's Feast
March 15, 1679

CANTO XXXXV
Annunciation: 1679

Angel Gabriel to *Mary* announced,
       The *Holy Spirit* birth,
Kateri on this day pronounced,
       A vow...sublime its worth.

Kateri's life seen as whole,
       Retaining chastity,
A lily-blossom in her soul,
       Exquisite tapestry,

As sun doth set in the sky,
       Multi-colors spreading,
When *God's Son* within her lie,
       Her glowing told her their wedding.

In ecstasy her soul united
       With her *Bridegroom Host,*
The fire within her had ignited,
       For *Him* she burned most.

At this *Mass...Annunciation*,
       Heaven's angels sang,
Kateri's vow...consummation,
       Alleluias rang!

Kateri surrendered ostentation,
       Wore a shawl of blue,
Apparent was renunciation,
       "Indian nun"...French knew!

Jesus Christ her *Princely Spouse,*
  Forever be *His* Bride,
Her vow in splendor did arouse,
  God's Love...glorified!

Of perpetual virginity the Princess gave,
  A jewel in crown rare,
Renouncing married love so brave,
  'Neath *Mary's mantle* fair.

In private made a consecration,
  To *Mother* so **Divine**,
Kateri's love on *Annunciation*,
  Enrapture so sublime!

Kateri's mother from Heaven
sent,
  Rays of jubilation,
Lily of the Iroquois nation,
  Pride resplendent!

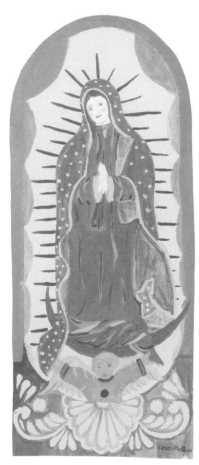

Tess Mullins, 16

CANTO XXXXVI
Increased Mortifications

Kateri's family returned from camp,
      Before the Virgin's feast,
Upon seeing her...emotions sank,
      Her health had all but ceased.

Shocked to see her skeletal,
      Body...emaciated,
Her spirit shone through eyes so well,
      Our Lord she radiated.

"Do not worry dear family,
      Affirmed Kateri,
My muscles work totally,
      I'll labor earnestly."

They shared her joy when vow she made,
      Kateri...*decreasing,*
While *Jesus*...homage to *Him* she paid,
      He with her...*increasing,*

When Kateri and Teresa met,
      After long separation,
The soul-mates with joyful tears wept,
      Talked with exultation.

Theresa burst with congratulations,
      For Kateri...her vow,
She was filled with admiration,
      Blessed her on her brow.

The two friends made declarations,
  To love *God* with greater zeal,
To triple their mortifications,
  In prayer they made a seal.

Kateri swept with *Love Divine,*
  At *Eucharist* adoration,
Her fervent prayer...gift sublime,
  Of intimate communication.

What seethed deep into her heart,
  Poured out in sighs and tears,
Heavenly sweetness she did impart,
  Her holy heart He hears.

Kateri loved *God* beyond extreme,
  For suffering she thirst,
The slightest fault, a crime so mean,
  She judged herself the worst.

Touched by huge blunt nails three,
  An image of her sin,
Which fixed *Jesus* to *His Tree,*
  That man, *His Body* win.

With each wound and spasm pain,
  The trickling of *His blood,*
Convulsive agony did not wane,
  His *mercy* gushed like flood.

Once when a branch hit Kateri's head,
  Threw her to the ground,
"*God* saved my life...she had said,
  Soul's penance I have found."

Kateri's head throbbed with *His,*
  She plunged to *His abyss,*
His Father's will, He'd not resist,
  Suffering was *her* bliss.

The garden of Gethsamani,
        Began *Paschal Mystery,*
Christ sweat tears of agony,
        "Spend one hour with me!"

On *Christ's shoulder* she reflected,
        His flesh so lacerated,
His *Sacred Wound*...bone detected,
        For sins He expiated.

In secrecy for one whole year,
        They scourged before confession,
To endure such pain, they had no fear,
        Such penance...their expression.

They'd begin with *act of Contrition*
        With whips of thorns in hand,
Then offer suffering for sin's remission,
        To purify the land.

For the *Cross* which crushed *His shoulder,*
        To Golgotha from Calvary,
Kateri knelt till lashings over,
        Begging *"Exert more energy!"*

When blood poured out and raw the skin,
        Senses felt suppression,
God-man Saviour...Life within,
        Then ready for...*confession.*

In time, Kateri began to wilt,
        She was feeling weak,
Theresa blamed herself for guilt,
        The *Blackrobe* she would seek.

He scolded them though reasons knew,
        "You have gone too far,
God knows your hearts for *Him* are true,
        Do not your bodies scar!"

"Your penance should be moderate,
       Your blood you should not shed,
Our dear Lord you can venerate,
       In you *His Life* be fed."

Theresa, truly in remorse,
       For Kateri so dear,
She promised priest a different course,
       And shed a heart-felt tear.

Kateri was forced to rest,
       With fever and stomach pain,
Two weeks later...ill health arrest,
       Then on her feet again.

Burning Love

Deirdre Wood, 7

CANTO XXXXVII
Burning Love

Her strength revived to her *Prince* went,
  To *Jesus love* and *Friend*,
To tell Him how much to her He meant,
  And ask for grace *He'd send.*

Transfixed upon the *Cross* He hung,
  With grief her tears were shed,
A lover's song to her was sung,
  "*My heart* for you has bled."

Tears of penitence did flow,
  From Kateri's broken heart,
Her *Beloved* withered so,
  His eyes with love did spark.

The torture of first jolt she felt,
  As *Christ* was hoisted up,
In homage to her *Spouse* she knelt,
  She'd drink *His* bitter cup.

The soldiers stretching *Christ*, she saw,
  On two wooden beams,
He died to bring love's precious law,
  Contradiction...seems.

Health restored...penances resumed,
  Though Kateri still weak,
Moderation...so attuned,
  Her love soared to peak.

Kateri in secret would perform,
       Penance to suffer pain,
So sinner's souls would reform,
       For *God, His Heaven* gain.

With sagamité she mixed ash,
       For *Jesus* she did fast,
To suffer for *His* every lash,
       That souls for *God* would last.

Throughout the months that did ensue,
       Kateri and Theresa met,
Penitential acts they'd do,
       Their plan was firmly set.

In winter winds and freezing cold,
       Along riverbank they'd pray,
The rosary with hands enfold,
       For soul's eternal day.

To suffer torture of painful freeze,
       Barefoot on ice they'd walk
Every minute they would seize,
       To *Jesus Christ* would talk.

A bloodless pain...a blister burn,
       Kateri's scheme devise,
To *Christ* her seal of honor earn,
       No one could criticize.

A burning fagot from fire withdrew,
       On her foot she'd press,
As non-Christian tribes do,
       To a slave-girl's flesh.

Faint was Kateri from this ordeal,
       To *Jesus* offered pain,
The maiming took some time to heal,
       Souls for *Him* she'd gain.

When Anastasia did complain,
     Kateri said, "Child's play...
Compared to my *Saviour's pain.*"
     What could her mother say?

To show *Our Lady* a token of love,
     Deep in snow the rosary prayed,
Sinking to her waist above,
     A walk round field she made.

When Father Cholenec "imprudent" said,
     "Quite natural," she did tell,
"To discuss with you my rosary tread,
     Escaped my thinking well."

Once again Kateri's health had altered,
     To Chapel she had to drag herself,
Trying to kneel she swayed and faltered,
     Leaving, she staggered-self.

She remembered *Jesus' fall,*
     So weak *He* could not stand,
With *His Cross* she heard *His call,*
     He gave His loving Hand.

CANTO XXXXVIII
Fall: 1679

Worn out by sacrifice extreme,
    Slowed down by fever slight,
Kateri exhausted...never did seem,
    To hide *God's radiant Light.*

Her eyes still glowed with *Love Divine,*
    Her voice with tone so low,
Sang, *"Thou art forever mine,"*
    Though her pace was slow.

The Fall had come with Autumn's glow,
    The pumpkins all were ripe,
The *Cross* from which *Christ's love* doth flow,
    Was her support and life.

As she from field and Church did go,
    Struggled with her stride,
She a Princess failing so,
    Knelt by her *Prince's side.*

Soon the leaves from trees will fall,
    The pumpkins will be gone,
Mother Earth will heed *God's call,*
    And Winter winds will mourn.

To daily Mass as magnet drawn,
    Kateri stumbling went,
Leaning against the pew each morn,
    To get her nourishment.

In front of the *Blessèd Sacrament*,
    Kateri transported knelt,
Immovable as if to Heaven sent,
    A burning love she felt.

A *Blackrobe* priest of Kateri did know,
    Observed at *adoration*,
From flame within...her face aglow,
    Transfiguration!

Her faith had attraction strong,
    To children big and small,
Grace-filled *Kateri's Band* was born,
    With her they would not fall.

Enita's young son at six, expired.
    While at the cemetery,
"Where will be your grave," inquired,
    A friend of Kateri?

"There," she said with a smile,
    Pointing to a spot,
All did laugh with some beguile,
    Prophetic was the lot.

Six months later when Kateri died,
    "This her grave would be,"
Unknowing...priest mystified,
    Picked by Kateri!

More and more to death she turned,
    To eternity,
She was worried...her soul churned,
    "What is my *destiny?*"

CANTO XXXXIX
A Peek Into Her Soul

When Kateri at the Chapel knelt,
    Into her soul did peek,
Many questions she had dealt,
    For perfection she did seek.

To be holy she did strive,
    To love *God* infinitely,
By *Jesus* and His *Cross* she'd rise,
    To Heaven eternally.

Statue of Kateri Tekakwitha on
the Great Bronze Doors of Saint
Patrick's Cathedral, New York City

"Kateri Examines Conscience"

Did I ever *God* offend?
 Enough time praying did I spend?
Were my penances always pleasing?
 Were any acts to *God* displeasing?
To poor and sick, show love and care?
 For desperate sinners offer prayer?
Did I bring many souls to *God?*
 Give good example for my *Lord?*
Did I waste *God's precious time?*
 Did I adore my *God Divine...*
To the fullest...love sublime?
 Did I love *You* unceasingly...
In humility and charity?
 Did I live my faith so true...
Bring young and old to *You?*
 "Please dear *Jesus*, calm my soul,
To see *Your Face* is my goal,
 Give me mercy...my sins forgive,
You've been my life...
 In death I'll live.

Kateri meditated on His Crown of Thorns   *Face of Christ*
©Marlene McCauley

CANTO XXXXX
Kateri's Passion

When March arrived, bird's winged their way,
    Again to the North,
Kateri gripped with pain this day,
    Visited her *Betrothed*.

Frequent vomiting and headache pain,
    A fever that did soar,
Harsh penances were to blame,
    Via Dolorosa to Chapel door.

A struggle back to longhouse made,
    To *Christ's Cross* she clung,
"Farewell" to her *Beloved*, she bade,
    Her *Passion* had begun.

Never again would Kateri walk,
    Confined to cot was she,
'Twas Lent when her sickness fought,
    She suffered agony.

She nailed herself upon the *Cross*,
    Once called the *Jesus Tree,*
Throbbing head as she did toss,
    Singing rosary.

Racked with pain she meditated,
    On His crown of thorns,
Through *Christ's Head* they penetrated,
    He suffered for man's wrongs.

Though deathly ill, with joy she dwell,
    With *Jesus crucified,*
A *Saviour-King...His* love did tell,
    She would be *purified.*

Her heart broken for man's vice,
    Two thieves *Christ* hung between,
To Dismas, "Today you'll be in Paradise,"
    His words...a piercing beam."

His parched lips and tongue she saw,
    Cleaving to *His jaw,*
Kateri heard *His cry, "I thirst,"*
    Her zeal for sinners burst.

While Kateri in contemplation,
    A priest did visit her,
On the dying...His exhortation,
    She listened...not a stir.

"Your suffering can be mortified,
    Smiling, she gasped and sighed,
That souls confess and be baptized,
    For *Jesus Crucified."*

"Plant a seed...the flower takes root,
    Your offering is a gift,
For sinners it will bear rich fruit,"
    His plea, a happy lift.

"By the *Cross* I was born,
    By it I'll live and die,
I offer my poor body worn,
    That souls will multiply!"

The heart that once in health had given,
    All to sick and poor,
Now in failing time was driven,
    Her suffering to endure.

Father Chauchêtière, an idea he found,
　　To keep Kateri happy,
He brought children to surround,
　　While teaching *faith-story*.

The children to Kateri were drawn,
　　They gave her an embrace,
Father led them in prayer each morn,
　　They saw *God* in her face.

A twinkle in her eye did tell,
　　Of her jubilation,
To see the children learning well,
　　She was wrapped in fascination.

The priest, his paintings did portray,
　　God's Majesty and awe,
Presenting a colorful display,
　　Of *His eternal law*.

Pictures of *Saints* and faith glory,
　　The Babe in the Virgin's arm,
Her Son in same arms at Calvary,
　　Ever guiding them from harm.

When host of *Angels* they did see,
　　They giggled merrily,
They loved *Angel Guardian's* beauty...
　　A mystical mystery!

When the priest with blessing left,
　　With joyful tears she wept,
Through the children, *God* she met,
　　With peaceful heart she slept.

CANTO XXXXXI
FRAGILE FADING FLOWER

The mockingbird so faint its trill,
      Hosannas soon to ring,
'Twas Saturday...*Palm Vigil,*
      The *Lenten Moon of Spring.*

The saintly girl lay so weak,
      The *Cross* she did caress,
Praying Village...air so bleak,
      She smiled...nonetheless.

Anastasia gave her love and care,
      Theresa knelt in prayer,
During day while field they tend,
      To Kateri...the *Spirit* send.

Happy to be in contemplation,
      Filled with gratitude,
Enflamed with love...her immolation,
      Alone in solitude.

To think of *God*...she did employ,
      As day and night she lay,
To see *His Holy Face*...her joy,
      A glimpse of Heaven's day.

She made the stations of the Cross,
      For *Jesus crucified,*
Declining strength to her no loss,
      Kateri...*sanctified.*

A *Holy Family* nurse was sent,
       To be with her all night,
Angels hovering o'er her bed spent,
       Keeping watchful light.

When Kateri asked if she could fast,
       Monday of *Holy Week,*
"Your time is coming to the last,
       A little you **must** eat!"

A happy smile transformed her face,
       A few spoonfuls she ate,
Soon her *Jesus* she would embrace,
       She, her *angel* would take.

She saw her *Saviour* in *Passiontide*,
       Clasping scepter-reed,
In seamless cloak *blasphemied*,
       His crown for man did bleed.

As she lay she saw her *King*,
       For *Him,* her offering,
For sinners she would expiate,
       Soon her death to consummate.

Holy Tuesday...the time drew near,
       Death waiting at her door,
Father Cholenec filled with fear,
       Soon Kateri would be no more.

For this fragile, fading flower,
       With *Jesus*, he'd return,
The priest would be back in one hour,
       A gift her soul did yearn.

When she heard his love announcement,
       Communion he would bring,
Her treasure...*Blessèd Sacrament*,
       Made her spirit sing.

Her family from the field would come,
      In time to celebrate,
So *Jesus* would have a *warm* welcome,
      All would venerate.

Kateri to her dearest friend,
      When both were left alone,
"I have no dress to depend,
      When *Jesus* enters home."

"Father Cholenec will soon be here,
      My clothes I gave away,
Do you have a dress my dear,
      For this *Sacred* day?"

Theresa helped Kateri dress to win...
      Her *Jesus-Spouse* so true,
A nice new dress of brown deerskin,
      With a blouse of blue.

Her face and hands did Theresa clean,
      Combed her hair awhile,
The Princess for her *Prince* did beam,
      Waiting with a smile.

Repeating words of preparation,
      With folded hands she lay,
Consumed her *Jesus* with devotion,
      Within her *He* did stay.

Her eyes closed in recollection,
      In ecstasy was she,
The priest left to hear confession,
      In prayer...her family.

Theresa held vigil for her that night,
      Heard Kateri's words of love,
Struggling with all her might,
      With wisdom from above.

265

Whispering with thoughts so faint,
      To Theresa she did tell,
"Keep striving to be a *saint*,
      Practice penance well."

"I'm sad to leave you, loyal friend,
      Gifts from *Heaven* I'll send,
Thank you for your help and love,
      We'll meet in *Paradise* above."

"To *Jesus* always remain loyal,
      Separate from Satan's foil,
Avoid those who do not love *God*,
      With the righteous...trod."

"Be good example in this land,
      In your prayer expand,
The name of *Jesus* with love invoke,
      Keep your faith-filled hope.

Theresa by her bed did sob,
      While Kateri tried to sleep,
She stroked her hand...spoke to *God*,
      "Bless my friend so sweet."

Her stomach racked with grueling pain,
      As friends came and went,
A smile she gave without feign,
      Weak voice...detriment

God showered Kateri with Mystical Gifts

"Kateri's Mystical Gifts"

A mystical light that shone so bright,
　　God gave to Kateri,
Spiritual incision interior vision,
　　God gave to Kateri,
Gifts while dying kept multiplying,
　　God gave to Kateri,
She picked out her grave, all were amazed,
　　God gave to Kateri,
She knew when she'd die, to Heaven fly,
　　God gave to Kateri,
She felt unworthy through life, by death ...gifts thrice,
　　God gave to Kateri,
She knew she could pray from Heaven each day,
　　God gave to Kateri,
A friend she could see, scourging unmercifully,
　　God gave to Kateri,
So she would be, with *Him* eternally,
　　God gave to Kateri,
When she was re-born...her face shone,
　　God gave to Kateri,
All pockmarks gone...her skin transformed,
　　God gave to Kateri,
Her face resplendent, *God's love transcendent,*
　　God gave to Kateri,
Healings she'd shower from *Eucharist power,*
　　Graces bestowing...love flowing,
To her friends on earth, she shares her mirth,
　　Answer their prayer with love and care,
Kateri's advice: pray... sacrifice,
　　Let *Eucharist* and *Cross* shine...
With *God's love* sublime,
　　Let your love *SOAR,*
　　Jesus Adore!
　　More
　　More
　　And More!

269

Kateri receives Jesus for the last time   *Jamie Jakubcyzk, 16*

CANTO XXXXXII
Kateri's Death to Life Preparation

The next day at the break of dawn,
    A black cloud seen in sky,
All of nature seemed to mourn,
    The *lily* soon to die.

As Kateri on her bed did lie,
    Wednesday of *Passion Week*,
She knew that soon her soul would fly,
    Her *Jesus* she would meet.

A friend of hers to woodland went,
    For scourging sacrifice,
Much energy she painfully spent,
    For Kateri's *peace-demise*.

"I'll recommend you to *God*,"
    Kateri spoke humbly,
You whipped yourself with rod,
    That my soul be free."

God gave Kateri a mystical eye,
    Of visionary light,
"I'll pray for you from *Heaven's height,*"
    The group for her did cry.

She urged them all to leave for work,
    She still had some time,
The crops you must never shirk,
    She promised to be fine.

The lodge emptied...they left in peace,
	Kateri closed her eyes,
The priest felt that soon she'd cease,
	She breathed heavy sighs.

For *Holy Viaticum,* he made preparation,
	Usually in Chapel done,
For Kateri he'd make exception,
	Jesus to Kateri's lodge would come.

'Twas the custom in the *Village of Prayer,*
	To Chapel...carried sick on a plank,
But not for Kateri...their *lily rare,*
	She to *God* did thank!

Theresa called from plantation,
	For *Last Rites* invocation,
The priest came for Kateri's anointing,
	With all *God's love* appointing.

The *Holy Trinity*, he did invoke,
	Father, Son and Holy Ghost,
The *Holy Oil* on her forehead pressed,
	The *Holy Cross* on her he blessed.

Kateri kissed her crucifix,
	Sighed, "*Jesus*, I love you,"
Her once rosy lips from being sick
	Then were ashen hue.

When the priest, *Jesus* pronounced,
	Her suffering lines ceased,
Expression of joy on her face announced,
	Jesus' love, her lease.

When she received her *Jesus-King,*
	She felt her soul restored,
The *angels* round her bed did sing,
	Her soul to *Heaven* soared!

Kateri Lemmon, 15

CANTO XXXXXIII
THE MIRACLE -April 17, 1680

At two-thirty, Matin's bells did toll,
  For the faithful all,
To pray for Kateri's loving soul,
  In peace, she'd hear *God's* call.

The *Holy Wednesday* service at four,
  God's mercy they'd implore,
From prayerful hearts, *God's love* would pour,
  So Kateri's soul would soar!

By Kateri's bed, two priests knelt,
  Theresa held her hand,
Silence reigned...*God's presence* felt,
  He was in command.

"Jesus, Mary," last words said,
  Her life-blood ebbed away,
Kateri's soul rose...body *dead*,
  Last breath at three, Wednesday.

When this fragile flower fell,
  Midway in Passiontide,
A glow transfiguring her face did tell,
  That *Christ* was at her side.

All the Mission with joy they cried,
  To know their *lily...glorified*,
Vigil of two sacred days,
  Eucharist and Cross...Kateri's praise.

Her very body's mortification,
  Crucible for soul's purification,
Rewarded by *God* ...sanctification,
  Heaven...summit of glorification.

"She was ripe for Heaven," the *Blackrobes* said,
  "In brief space of time, many souls led,"
Graces from Kateri...her loving endeavors,
  Cross and *Eucharist*...her spiritual treasures.

Angels in Heaven sang with glee,
  The Song of Kateri,
Princess of the *Eucharist*...pure Lily,
  With her *Prince*...eternally.

Kateri Tekakwitha...*God's love* she'll bind,
  Gifts from Him...for you she'll find,
Virtues...jewels for emulating,
  God-filled Lily...self-effacing.

Dear *Mohawk Lily*...beyond compare,
  Fill us with your fragrant prayer,
Unite us in *God's brilliant light,*
  Let us strive to your great height!

Kateri Tekakwitha,
  God's effervescent star,
Humble maiden...free of mar,
  Your sainthood shines not afar!

Kateri sighed, Jesus I love you! scupture, Marlene McCauley

The following is an excert taken from a letter of Father Pierre Cholenec, one of Kateri's spiritual advisors, on the death of the holy maiden. It was written May 1, 1680.

"She died as she lived, that is to say, as a saint. Such she was regarded here by all the village before and after her death..."
Positio, Fordham Press
New York, 1940

Shortly after Kateri's death, a granite tombstone was erected over her gravesite which contains the following inscription.

Kateri Tekakwitha
April 17, 1680
ONKWE-ONWE-KE KATSITSIIO TEIOTSITSIANEKARON
(Kateri Tekakwitha, the most beautiful flower that bloomed among the Indians.)

Tree of Peace

Epilogue

Her soul took flight as a butterfly,
    United her Prince in Heaven high,
Transported at last...her eternal home,
    Flooded with light at Our Father's Throne,
By mystical love, she was sated with bliss,
    Her mother's welcome with a sweet kiss...
Though *Kateri's Song* came to an end,
    A symphony of love she would send,
Our Princess fulfilled her earthly mission,
    Six days after death...a first apparition.
To Father Chauchétiere...a clear direction,
    To tell how her life was her death's resurrection,
To paint her image as he saw Kateri,
    So all would know God by her life's victory,
When appeared to him two times more,
    She provided prophecy and wisdom galore,
To Anastasia who guided her soul to great height,
    Saw Kateri engulfed in brilliant light,
"The cross was my life and my death's glory,
    The cross should be *your* life's story,"
She, preparing her "auntie" for a heavy cross,
    The death of her son...a brutal loss,
To her friend Teresa, she did impart,
    Words of hope from her Divine heart,
"Only for Heaven you must strive,"
    Teresa knew Kateri...much alive!"
Cures fell like a shower below,
    Whatever help needed from this saintly soul,
From the *Village of Prayer* to France, she became,
    "Star of the New World"...Lily Mohawk fame,
Earth from her grave or the cross she wore,
    The plate which she ate from, relics and more,
Miraculous cures, favors for all,
    Gifts from Heaven...her call,
Animals diseased...friends near death's door,
    Healings from Heaven...much to adore.

Her promise made...a golden seal,
 The *soul* first...then body she'll heal.
Her mission of love will never cease,
 Bringing all to the Eucharist, His joy and His peace.
Her role of uniting all brothers to God,
 Race, creed or color, all one with the Lord.
She, the saint of the Redskin race,
 Will forever protect in God's embrace.
For the *Lily of the Mohawks*...this proclamation,
 Reward by the Church...Beatification,
Destined soon for Canonization!
 We invite you to see our Princess *crowned*,
A *"Blessed"* on earth...Heavens graces abound!

1656-1680

PART IV

The
Beatification
Of
Kateri Tekakwitha
"Lily of the Mohawks"

To witness a great moment in history
when an Iroquois virgin from
the Eastern woodland
of newborn America
received her crown
as "Blessed."

Commemorating the twenty-fifth Anniversary of the
Beatification of Kateri Tekakwitha on June 22, 1980, by Pope
John Paul II at St. Peter's Basilica in Rome, Italy.

@Marlene McCauley, 2005

Beatification Ceremony of Kateri Tekakwitha
St. Peter's Basilica, Rome, Italy, 1980

POSTLUDE

Heaven's bells pealed a tune,
> On the twenty-second day of June,
Of the nineteen-eighty glowing moon,
> To exalt a humble maiden soon!

'Twas three hundred years this soul took flight,
> To be born of eternal light.
Her promise, "I will pray for you,"
> Heeded to many the centuries through.

Generations twelve, prayed for this day,
> Marked by *God's providential ray,*
The sun delivered a golden beam,
> Kateri elevated...was it a dream?

Exultant hearts did overflow,
> As toward *Mother Church* their steps did go,
Native Americans resplendently dressed,
> To see their sister at last made "Blest!"

Left to right: Msgr. Paul Lenz, Dir. of Black and Indian Missions, Washington, D.C.; Cardinal Cooke, N.Y.; Cardinal Krol, Philadelphia; Fr. Joseph, McBride, S.J., U.S. Vice-Postulator

Swiss guards at St. Peter's Door, Meeting people by the score.
Beatification, June 22, 1980

Swiss guards at St. Peter's door,
      Meeting people by the score,
Standing stately...sword in hand,
      Pilgrims passing from every land.

Twenty-five thousand flocked to see,
      An outstanding moment in history,
To each a missalette...then a seat,
      The Kateri group...left transcept did meet.

From everywhere...all came to see,
      Five "Venerables" made "Beati,"
Two sons of Spain...two of France,
      All of missionary stance.

Lived within a hundred fifty years,
      Filled with faith, they had no fears,
Each accepted *Christ's* invitation,
      Peter Betancur to Marie of the Incarnation.

In their souls His grace did fill,
     Joseph Ancieta..."Apostle of Brazil,"
Bishop Laval...the "first" of Quebec,
     Kateri Tekakwitha...of the Mohawk "sect.'

Heroic virtue...their call,
     Proclaiming *Christ's gospel* to all,
In distant lands and Indian soil,
     Midst suffering, they did toil!

Americans and Guatemalans,
     Canadians and Brazilians,
Assembled for the beatification,
     A Pontifical celebration!

Beatification Mass at St. Peter's in Rome, June 22, 1980

Beatification Mass at St. Peter's in Rome, June 22, 1980

St. Peter's Basilica...awe-inspiring,
　　　　Spaciousness...Wreathed columns spiraling,
Canopied altar...the golden throne,
　　　　Above which soars Michelangelo's dome.

Imposing edifice...Christendom's rock,
　　　　Crypt of St. Peter...under this spot,
Antiquity-rooted...apostolic succession,
　　　　Introducing the solemn procession!

One of the concelebrants of the day,
　　　　Jesuit General...Father Arrupé,
Bishops, "Arch,"...Cardinal, too
　　　　Took their places on cue.

Wearing red and violet zuchetti,
　　　　Soon they knew the moment ready!
Lights went on...the organ resounded,
　　　　Pope John Paul II, to the alta

An endearing soul...filled with love,
　　　　Missionary spirit...Poland's dove,
Christ's vicar...the Spirit's prize,
　　　　Pope John Paul II...with *"talking eyes!"*

'Twas an impressive, stirring sight,
    At the Penitential rite,
When the members did arrive,
    To petition their candidates five.

Silence reigned...Bishop Hubbard's talk,
    "Please count as "Blessed,"...Kateri, a Mohawk!"
Hearts beat in anticipation,
    For the Holy Father's declaration.

In robes of glimmering white and gold,
    The silver staff, his hand did hold,
Just before the Gloria rite,
    Announcement made from the altar's height.

Bishop Howard Hubbard
& Pope John Paul II at
Kateri's beatification

"By apostolic authority,
    Declare that Venerable Kateri,
Will henceforth be called, '*Blest,*'"
    Her life a miracle...severe the test!

"April seventeenth...the feast,"
    The day her heartbeat ever ceased,
A thunderous applause echoed through,
    Hearty clapping only grew!

Leading to a mighty roar,
      Vibrating the massive *"holy door!"*
Tears welled in many eyes,
      Ecstasy...hard to disguise!

Indian people burst with pride,
      To see their own beatified!
Hearts cried in exultation,
      On this day of jubilation!

Blessed Kateri...God's love she'll bind,
      Gifts from Him...for you she'll find,
Virtues...jewels for emulating,
      God-filled "Lily"...self-effacing!

The Sistine choir...Gregorian sang,
      In Latin phrases their voices rang!
"Missa de Angelis"...ethereal cadence,
      Heavenly tones...mystical radiance!

Fathers Thomas Egan, S.J. and Henri Béchard, S.J.

"He-Who-Consoles-
The-Mind"
(Father Thomas E. Egan, S.J.)

with "Between-
Two-Skies"
(Father Henri Béchard, S.J.)

A Seminarian from Albany
    Gave the reading splendidly,
"Your love and works are your worth,
    You are the salt of the earth!"

"Princess White Dove" from Caughnawaga,
    An Iroquois mission in Canada,
Spoke the petition in Mohawk tongue,
    Her chanting tones strongly rung!

"Let *Christ's* love be your leaven!"
    Her beautiful voice reached Heaven!
For St. Peter's...an innovation,
    In native dialect...this recitation!

Our Holy Father's homily,
    Ending with our Kateri,
Praised her faith to God above,
    His sacred *Cross*...her deepest love.

Princess White Dove, a
Mohawk from
Kahnawake, St. Francis
Xavier Mission

*Spoke the petition in the
Mohawk tongue
Her chanting tones
strongly rung!*

Three Indian sisters in Rome

Msgr. Paul A Lenz with Sr. Gloria Davis, S.B.S. (Navajo Reservation - Arizona)

The Honorable Robert Wagner {center}, U.S. Envoy to the Vatican, hosted a party for the pilgrims on their arrival in Rome. Also in the picture are Cardinal Baum of Washington, Cardinal Cooke of New York, and Cardinal Krol of Philadelphia. Cardinal Krol is President of the Bureau of Catholic Indian Missions and was the spiritual leader of the American Indian Pilgrimage to Rome.

"Through suffering, she did impart,
    Resignation and joyful heart!"
"Last words as she bid adieu,"
    Jesus...I love You!"

Presentation of gifts...a spectacular sight,
    Indians dressed in regalia bright,
From United States and Canada,
    In line...approached the altar.

Fathers Bechard and Joseph McBride,
    Observing this filled with pride,
Vice-Postulators for Kateri,
    And the General...Father Molinari!

Director of "Missions"...Monsignor Lenz,
    Happily watched his many friends,
Arrayed in full ceremonial dress,
    Beads and buckskins to feathered headdress!

Potawatomi and Saketon,
    To countless tribes, they did belong!
Cherokee, Choctaw and Papago,
    Blackfoot, Laguna and Navajo!

The Sioux, Tewa and Mohawk,
    Deafening applause as each did walk!
Ben Black Bear and Chief Delisle,
    An entourage through the aisle.

Francis Hairy Chin and Iron Eyes,
    Camera clicking to immortalize!
Big Chief Jim Shot Both Sides,
    Expressing homage of the tribes.

"To the great Holy White Father," he read,
    Presenting a jeweled band for the head!
Hopi pottery...in sienna and while,
    Kachina dolls...a colorful sight!

Native American with Cardinal Krol and Billy Antone (Tucson)

Iron Eyes cody of TV fame

Anne Dyer & Iron Eyes

Papago baskets and a peace pipe,
     A Navajo rug with a bright stripe,
Jewelry made of brilliant seeds,
     Wampum belts of vivid beads!

Tortoise Clan

With no concern for protocol,
     The Holy Father talked to all!
"Little Peacock, gave a stole,
     "See the *"Lily,"*...Kateri's symbol!"

Look...the turtle, wolf and bear!"
     "Thank you for beatifying...Kateri fair!"
Pope John Paul II blessed her there,
     For all...a memorable affair!"

A beautiful Mass...the morning long,
     The entire Basilica broke in song,
"Holy God, we praise Thy name,"
     Blessèd Kateri forever reign!

Bear Clan

After the Mass, the Pope did greet,
     Each representative gathered to meet,
In the chapel of St. Sebastian,
     Spirit and love-light never dim!

Wolf Clan

Deacon Spears

297

The blessings complete...he left his seat,
     A message of love from the Papal Suite,
The *Angelus bells* o'er Rome were heard,
     "Be it done unto me...The holy word!"

From the Basilica to the square,
     Pope John Paul's words...filled the air,
An afterglow...on each one's face,
     Knowing that Kateri, he did embrace.

In parting the Holy Father did bless,
     The Indians of Canada and the U.S.
Oh Blessèd Kateri...for all mankind,
     A sweet bouquet for earth you'll find!

Dear Mohawk *"Lily,"*...beyond compare!
     Fill us with your fragrant prayer,
Unite us in *God's brilliant light,*
     Let us strive to your great height.

Blessèd Kateri Tekakwitha,
     God's effervescent star,
Humble maiden...free of mar,
     Your sainthood shines not afar!

With no concern for protocol, The Holy Father talked to all -

Fr. Joseph McBride, S.J., Mary-Eunice, Marlene
A message of love from the Papal Suite

An afterglow on each one's face
Marlene, Peter and Native American

The Holy See has approved this Mass prayer which may be used on the Feast of Blessed Kateri Tekakwith:

Lord God, you called the virgin, Blessed Kateri Tekakwitha, to shine among the Indian people as an example of innoncence of life. Through her intercession, may all peoples of every tribe, tongue, and nationa, having been gathered into your Church, proclaim your greatness in one song of praise. We ask this through our Lord Jesus christ, Your Son, who lives and reigns with yo and the Holy Spirit one God, for ever and ever.

Kateri Prayer

O God, who among the many marvels of Your Grace in the New World, did cause to blossom on the banks of the Mohawk and of the St. Lawrence, the pure and tender Lily, Kateri Tekakwitha, grant we beseech You, the favor we beg through her intercession; (your request) that this Young Lover of Jesus and of His Cross may soon be counted among the Saints of Holy Mother Church, and that our hearts may be enkindled with a stronger desire to imitate her innocence and faith. Through the same Christ Our Lord. Amen.

Our Father and Hail Mary once, and Glory be to the Father, three times.

IMPRIMATUR: Most Rev. Bishop Howard Hubbard, D.D.

July 14th Official Feast Day

Kateri's official feast day is celebrated on July 14. Originally, at her Beatification in Rome in 1980, Pope John Paul II designated April 17 (Kateri's death date) as her feast day, however, since it conflicted with Holy Week services, Bishop Howard Hubbard, D.D. of the Albany Diocese, petitioned the Holy Father to change it to July 14, the peak season for the Kateri Shrines.

In parting the Holy Father did bless the Indians of Canada & the U.S.

APPENDICES

Mohawk Vocabulary

Aréskoi	= War god	
Arósen	= Squirrel	
assontaté	= please	
Akwesasne	= Where the partridge spreads its wings	

Enita	= Moon

Fort Oranje	= Albany

Gagósa	= evil spirit
Ganóshote	= Trotter's Dance

Iorágade	= Sunshine
Iowerano	= Cold Wind
Isda	= mother

Jesos Takwantor	= Jesus, have mercy on me.

Kahenta	= Meadow-flower
Karitha	= Cook
Kateri Tekakwitha	= Gah-de-lee Deh-gah-quee-tah

Nyâwen	= I thank you!

Okis	= demons
Okwiré	= Tree
Otsikéta	= Sugar

Rakeni	= Father (priest)
Raseroni	= French Catholics
Ravennio	= God (His word is law)

Segon	= I greet you!
Segon Skennon gowa!	= Welcome...Peace be with you!
Satekon	= Balance (Wife of Chief Ganeagowa)
Sewannio	= O God

Tawasonta	= cascades below Albany (Small river tumbles over ledges)
Tionnontoge	= main town of Mohawk people
Tsoniton-gówa	= Great Beaver

Kateri Shrines

Kateri's Birthplace

Auriesville, N.Y. 12016
National Kateri Center
Tekakwitha League Headquarters
Office of the Vice-Postulator
National Shrine of the North American Martyrs

Kateri's Baptisimal Site

Fonda, N.Y. 12068
Tekakwitha Memorial Chapel
Mohawk Indian Museum
Restored Mohawk Village of Caughnawaga

Kateri's Tomb

Kahnawake, P.Q.
C.P. 70
Quebec, Canada; JOL, IBO
St. Francis Xavier Mission Church
Home of World-Renowned Mohawk Choir
Office of the Canadian Vice-Postulator

Contemporary History

Sept. 19-25, 2004

The Smithsonian native American Museum opened officially with a grand reception and procession. A multitude of Kateri devotees as well as Mohawks from St. Regis, Kahnawake and N.Y. marched to honor Blessed Kateri (led by Sr. Kateri Mitchell, Mohawk nun and Executive Dir. of the Tekakwitha Conference).

Among 40,000 honored Native Americans, Kateri Tekakwithas plaque in bronze was placed in an area on the 4th level of the museum, due to efforts of Kateri photographer Anne Scheuerman.

A Kateri Shrine started by the late Osage Indian, Opal Rector, (Phoenix, Arizona) (while terminally ill with cancer) is

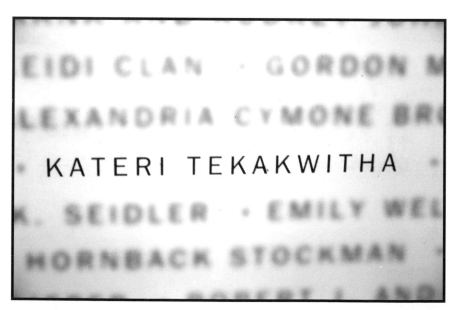

Bronze Plaque   *Photographer Anne Scheuerman*

Smithsonian Native American Museum on the Mall, Washington, D.C.

in progress on the grounds of the Immaculate Conception Church, Pawhuska, Oklahoma (Opal's Osage Territory).

The incredible plans include a 24' Native American steel crucifix (with designs symbolic of Kateri), a meditation garden, stations, of the cross, a waterfall and a life-sized statue of Blessed Kateri. When completed, it will be a magnet for drawing souls to Christ through Blessed kateri as well as placing the tiny village of Pawhuska on the map!

Because this year 2005 marks the 25th Anniversary of Kateri's beatification in Rome and the 325th Anniversary of her death, Bishop, Most Rev. Jacques Berthelet, CSV. of The Diocese of Longuevil, Canada declared a Jubilee year for the Mission of St. Francis Xavier in Kahnawake, Quebec, Canada.

In an effort to canonize Blessed Kateri, Msgr. Paul Lenz (Dir. of Black and Indian Missions, Washington, D.C.) initiated a national prayer campaign through Cardinals, Bishops and every Pastor in the US, to engage in a Triduum of prayer at the time of her feast day July 14, 2005, for the miracle needed for the Church's official declaration of Kateri's sainthood.

Biography of Author

Marlene & Allan at Lourdes, France 2004

Upon graduation from Emmanuel College, Boston, Mass. with a major in English and Theatre, Marlene ventured to New York to become an actress. Early on it appeared that she was well on her way, having been accepted for additional training at the prestigious Actor's Studio under the tutelage of Lee Strasberg.

God had other plans . . . for shortly thereafter, she met a charming Irishman and sensed she was falling love.

Recognizing that "love" might prove to be a stumbling block to her acting career, Marlene took a temporary assignment as a dancer with Ringling Bros. Barnum & Bailey which brought her to Sarasota, Florida, an adequate distance away from her new pal and further career interference.

The separation did not get the job done as the two were married six months later at St. Malachy's Actor's Chapel, in New York, by circus priest, Father Ed Sullivan and with Father Weiser concelebrating.

Now, forty-eight "plus" years, six children, thirteen grandchildren and hundreds of family theatre performances later, (many involving Kateri), we find Marlene having just completed this third book with Kateri being the ever present link between these writings and travels to most of the religious shrines of the world, wherein promotion of Kateri served as a prominent motivation.

Through the efforts of Marlene and the tens of thousands of other Kateri devotees throughout the world, our dear Blessed Kateri one day soon will be known as St. Kateri Tekakwitha.

Bibliography

Bachard, S.J. Fr. Henri, *Kateri Tekakwitha*, Kateri Center, Kahnawake, Quebec, (1994).

Bonvillain, Nancy, *The Mohawk*, Chelsea House, NY, (1991).

Graymont, Barbara, *The Iroquois*, Chelseo House, NY, (1988).

McCauley, Marlene, *Adventures with a Saint...Kateri Tekakwitha: Lily of the Mohawks*, Grace House, AZ, (1992).

Thwaites, Reuben G., *Jesuit Relations and allied documents*, ed. Cleveland, 1896-1901, 73 Vols.

The venerable servant of God, Kateri Tekakwitha, *Positio of the Historical Section of the Sacred Congregation of Rites*, Rome, English Edition, NY Fordham Press, (1940).

Weiser, S.J., Fr. Francis X., *Kateri Tekakwitha*, Kateri Center, Quebec, (1972).

To Order:

Song of Kateri...*Princess of Eucharist*
by Marlene McCauley

Please mail
$14.95 plus $4.00 for handling and shipping.
(Special discount for bulk orders).

TO:
Grace House Publishing
6237 N. 15th Street
Phoenix, AZ 85014
(602) 265-9151

Marlene is available to talk on Kateri Tekakwitha anywhere
throughout the U.S., Canada, Alaska & Hawaii,
Call (602) 265-9151.

Whitey, Marlene's cat helps her write her *Song of Kateri.* Whitey also assisted
Marlene at writing his own book *Whitey From Heaven: a Wondrous CAT*